CONTEN

THE COMPLETE CROCK POT EXPRESS MEAL PREP COOKBOOK

Jane Stuart

Warning-Disclaimer

The purpose of this book is to educate and entertain. The author or publisher does not guarantee that anyone following the techniques, suggestions, tips, ideas, or strategies will become successful. The author and publisher shall have neither liability or responsibility to anyone with respect to any loss or damage caused, or alleged to be caused, directly or indirectly by the information contained in this book.

INTRODUCTION

With today's generation of new foodies eager to explore new flavors mixed with traditional tastes, pressure cookers are back in fashion! Pressure cooking is not just another cooking method, this is a lifestyle that will dramatically improve your health and wellbeing. The Crock-Pot Express is a unique piece of kitchen equipment that makes entire dishes in minutes rather than hours. Besides being extremely practical, this cooker is a fun, affordable and innovative kitchen device for a modern household. This is one of the hottest culinary trends of 2018!

Thanks to the Crock-Pot Express, meal prep becomes a breeze since you can cook a large amount of food in a short period of time. A return to rustic dining, meal prep is one of the best ways to serve family meals and have plenty of alternatives. You will learn to make classic recipes such as Chili, Hummus, or Chicken soup, as well as fancy, innovative recipes such as Mug Cake or Vegan Mac & Cheese. From now onwards, you will be able to get all the nutrients you need and have the extra time for other activities.

If you find maintaining healthy eating habits and losing weight difficult, try a different approach. In this recipe collection, we simply connected healthy foods with meal prep and pressure cooking. Whether you're looking for classic recipes or recipes for a specific dietary regimen, you are sure to find a tremendous inspiration in this cookbook.

HOW DOES THE CROCK-POT EXPRESS WORK?

The Crock-Pot Express is a unique kitchen device designed to cook food under pressure. This multi-cooker can do the job of a pressure cooker, slow cooker, rice maker, yogurt maker, steamer, sauté pan, classic pot, and electric oven. Classic recipes such as pasta, chili or stew can be prepared in 15 to 30 minutes, from start to finish. Further, you can make French toast or whip up a bread pudding. You can make salads, fresh fruit desserts, snacks and appetizers, almost everything. Thanks to its built-in settings, the versatility of your Crock-Pot Express is amazing! Vegetarians and vegans, keto and gluten-free dieters, picky eaters and hedonists, we all love the Crock-Pot Express for its ability to cook one-pot meals in a flash. You don't have to soak dry beans and grains because they turn out great in the Crock-Pot Express.

The Crock-Pot Express is the next generation of kitchen appliance that uses steam and high temperature to create pressure inside the cooking chamber. It has an air-tight lid that locks into place; it is a smart way to preserve nutrients, achieve great flavors and stay on your household budget! The Crock-Pot Express protects the environment and saves your time too.

How does the Crock-Pot Express work? It has twelve fully automated cooking programs, which may be available depending on the model. These settings offer lots of flexibility in the kitchen.

SLOW COOK – this is the perfect program for gently simmering and slow cooking.

MEAT/STEW – as the name implies, you can use this program to cook meat and stew; it is especially useful for tough and cheap cuts of meat.

BEANS/CHILI – this setting is suitable for dry beans, grains, cereals, and desserts.

RICE/RISOTTO – you can cook all types of rice as well as porridges and oatmeal in a fraction of time.

STEAM – this is a great function for delicate vegetables and seafood.

DESSERTS – cakes, fudges and puddings are made easy with this program.

SOUP – you can cook an entire meal such as soup and stew using this setting.

BROWN/SAUTE – you can sauté vegetables, brown meats and thicken your sauces with this function; go one step further and use this function to maximize food's flavor on an easy way.

There are other intelligent programs such as MULTIGRAIN, POULTRY, YOGURT, and KEEP WARM.

5 REASONS WE LOVE THE CROCK-POT EXPRESS

1. Good eating habits are linked to a healthy life.

Your eating habits can affect your health and overall wellbeing which is why it is important to make good food choices. Cooking at home is a powerful key to healthfulness. Cooking at home can help you feel great and stay healthy and happy. Researchers have found that family dinners are an extremely important component of a healthy lifestyle.

Pressure cooking tends to preserve valuable nutrients better than conventional cooking methods; it also requires less fat and liquid, which can cause the greatest nutrient loss. Cook with the Crock-Pot Express and forget lack of energy levels, poor physical and mental health, obesity, and chronic diseases.

2. Because pressure cooking is better and cheaper.

If you want to eat better and stay on budget, the right kitchen tools may help you. The Crock-Pot Express can cook almost everything so you can save hundreds of dollars a year. This is one of the most convenient and the most affordable ways to cook a large amount of beans, grains, stocks and meats for future meals.

This "set it and forget" function has made cooking convenient and faster than ever! Moreover, your Crock-Pot Express will last for years!

3. It can significantly cut cooking time.

If you are way too tired to cook at the end of a long, busy day, look at it this way – try one of the best hands-off cooking methods that save plenty of time in the kitchen. The Crock-Pot Express utilizes a super-heated steam to cook your favorite meals faster than ever.

The Crock-Pot Express has a KEEP WARM feature so you can hold your meals at your desired serving temperature until you are ready for dinner. Therefore, you can cook when you find free time. Unlike conventional pots, ovens and cookers, you don't need to constantly monitor the Crock-Pot Express. Since it is self-regulated, your meals taste like you've been cooking all day. Shh! The Crock-Pot Express will keep your secret.

4. It's easy to use.

The Crock-Pot Express is a multi-use gadget that will change the way you cook. With so many settings, you will become obsessed with your new cooker, especially if you are an amateur chef. Seriously, The Crock-Pot Express makes a pot of grains in 10 to 15 minutes. The Crock-Pot Express does a great job of sautéing and searing before cooking so you will not need an extra pan. In addition, meat and vegetables come out evenly browned. An easy-to-read digital display is user-friendly and it makes cooking easier and more fun. The Crock-Pot Express is also safe since it automatically turns off and releases steam. It's easy to fall in love with a low-effort cooking!

5. The Crock-Pot Express is eco-friendly.

Sustainable eating is one of the biggest food trends in 2018. When it comes to energy waste and energy efficient cooking techniques, choose cookers that do not require a separate gas hobs or electric stoves. Simply choose a green cooking method. A quick cooking time means less energy use, which is beneficial for people and our planet. Go green, there is no Planet B!

MEAL PREP: TURN A CHORE INTO A LIFELONG HABIT

Wouldn't it be nice if you could find a simple way to plan and stick to a healthy diet? Cooking big batches of food in the Crock-Pot Express sounds like a great idea, right? Further, you can store these meals in the refrigerator or freezer for a long-term storage! This is meal prepping in a nutshell.

It might mean that you spend Sunday morning cooking several family meals for the upcoming week. The Crock-Pot Express allows you to prepare a large amount of food for faster and easier cooking later in the week. Preparing food in advance means spending less money on takeout and having more time for yourself. Meal prep can transform your life in a way you couldn't even imagine. Listed below are just a few of the benefits of meal prepping.

- Meal prep saves you time. Tons of time.

Making your food in advance is such a time saver for your busy schedule! Your dinner or lunch (even three and more) took just 50 minutes to make in the Crock-Pot Express on a Sunday afternoon! For instance, you can sauté a big batch of onions and vegetables and use them for several meals. You can make fish fillets and refrigerate them; they can last for 3 to 4 days in your refrigerator. Then, you can multitask and prepare a fish salad and chowder for the next week. Just make sure to pick a time you can devote to cooking and meal prep. Takeout? No thanks, life is much better when you have already got a lunch box with healthy foods. This routine will keep you feeling energized all day long, so you can boost your productivity.

- Your new routine saves you money.

Think of it this way: People spend thousands of dollars a year on takeout! Buying in bulk is the best way to save more money on your food budget. Another key is your freezer. It is great to have a healthy frozen meal on hand, ready to pop into the microwave or the Crock-Pot Express. Keep in mind that the best recipes for freezing include meats, chilies, stews, casseroles and similar foods. Foods that do not freeze well include dairy-based meals (with yogurt and sour cream), cooked egg whites, cooked meals with potatoes, cucumber, lettuce, fried foods and so on. Meal prep also reduces food waste because you always know what's in the refrigerator and freezer. Afterwards, you can pack your leftovers in the freezer and have a peace of mind.

- Meal prep will help you lose weight and stay healthy.

This is one of the greatest benefits of meal prep. Recent studies have found that meal prepping has both short and long term health benefits. Preparing homemade meals will give you an insight into calorie intake and help you control your food portions. By packing your own portions, you will be less likely to overeat.

Average restaurant meals contain too much sugar and salt as well as more calories than regular homemade meals? With meal prepping, you can control portion size, calories and ingredients in your recipes. No colors, additives and chemicals. Make time to sit down at the dinner table and you will set a great example for your kids. Studies have proven that adults and children who eat as a family are less likely to be overweight. In addition, meal prep can reduce stress, which can affect your physical and mental health.

6 SECRETS OF PEOPLE WHO MEAL PREP

1) Start small, then go bigger.

Cook big-batch recipes on the weekend and eat well for days. Pick a simple recipe like chicken; for instance, prepare 2 pounds of chicken breast and freeze them, so you can use them during the next week. You can also start with stocks and soups, it depends on your cooking skills. Just keep moving forward and you will become better and better in meal prepping. Once you master a small task in the kitchen, you will be able to take your favorite recipes and adapt them to be made in advance; it will be a huge motivation!

2) What should you prep? Meal prep strategies for breakfast, lunch, and dinner.

Here are some ideas for prep-friendly foods:

Breakfast – waffles, pancakes, muffins, hard-boiled eggs, granola, energy bars, smoothies, and chopped fruits.

Lunch – roasted vegetables, raw vegetables, leafy greens, meats, stews, beans, and soups.

Dinner – fish and seafood, cooked rice and quinoa, dressings and dips, cooked chicken, and fresh mirepoix,

Almost no one likes cooking in the morning. Therefore, you can make a big pot of instant oatmeal on Sunday afternoon; some topping ideas include chopped up apples and peaches, peanut butter, berries, cinnamon, yogurt. Therefore, you do not eat the same breakfast every morning. For lunch, you can make chicken bowls with rice, vegetables and spices; you can put it into grab and go mason jars and have three or four servings of the same meal. Of course, you can always save leftovers for tomorrow evening. For dinner, freezer meals are always a good idea, especially when you have one-pot meals that come together at the last minute with foods you already have in your pantry.

Make a big batch of a chili or old-fashioned stew in your Crock-Pot Express, sit back and relax.

3) Buy good-quality storage containers and freezer bags.

To refrigerate your meals, you can use aluminum pans, Pyrex bowls, Mason jars or glass dishes; you can cover them with plastic wrap to prevent foods from spoiling. Then, buy good Ziploc bags to prevent freezer burn and leakage. Here is a great trick: fill the bag with vegetables first, then place the layer of meat on top. Consider purchasing takeout-style containers and lunch boxes so you can eat direct from them. Win-win!

4) Plan a weekly menu.

You can get dinner on the table every night with a little pre-planning and a rough idea of what you'd like to prepare. You don't have to plan every single meal, just plan a few meals (multiple portions of staple foods) that you and your family would like to eat in the next week. Meal planning and batch cooking are one of the smartest ways to balance your diet and make good food choices every day! Enjoy this top-of-your-game feeling!

5) Focus on simple recipes.

Take shortcuts and avoid complicated recipes with a lot of ingredients. Double or triple the amount of food; in a hurry, opt for canned beans and chickpeas, pre-cut veggies and fruits, and frozen vegetable mix.

6) Cooking doesn't have to be boring.

Take advantage of this time and have a little fun with your family. Keep your kids entertained and turn cooking into a fun activity for them. Before you know it, you will be making the best family moments ever! You can listen to music or audio language learning programs too.

BREAKFAST

1. Autumn Apple Butter

Here is a simple and easy way to make pumpkin apple butter. Serve on freshly baked waffles, muffins or butter cookies.

Servings 8

Ready in about 15 minutes

NUTRITIONAL INFORMATION (Per Serving)

159 - Calories
3.1g - Fat
32.3g - Carbs
2.8g - Protein
22.7g - Sugars

Ingredients

- 1 can (15-ounce) can pumpkin puree
- 2 cups apple, cored and chopped
- 1 cup 100% apple juice
- 1 tablespoon apple pie spice
- 1/2 cup brown sugar
- 1/3 cup golden syrup
- 1/4 teaspoon ground allspice
- 1/8 teaspoon kosher salt

Directions

1. Place all of the above ingredients in your Crock-Pot Express.
2. Secure the lid and press the "SOUP" button. Press the "START/STOP" button; cook for 10 minutes at High pressure.
3. Once cooking is complete, use a natural pressure release and carefully remove the lid. Let cool completely.

Storing

- Spoon your apple butter into airtight containers; keep in the refrigerator for 1 to 2 weeks.
- To freeze, spoon your apple butter into airtight containers. Freeze up to 1 to 2 months. Defrost in the refrigerator. Enjoy!

2. Old-Fashioned Blackberry Jam

Here is a perfect breakfast or snack! Just toast a slice of crusty homemade bread and top with peanut butter and a dollop of grandma's blackberry jam. Yummy!

Servings 12

Ready in about
1 hour
15 minutes

NUTRITIONAL INFORMATION
(Per Serving)

122 - Calories
0.1g - Fat
30.7g - Carbs
1.5g - Protein
26.5g - Sugars

Ingredients

- 3 pounds blackberries, washed and cleaned
- 1/4 cup lemon juice
- 1/2 cup granulated sugar

Directions

1. Arrange blackberries in the Crock-Pot Express. Pour the lemon juice and sugar over the blackberries. Allow them to rest about 1 hour.
2. Secure the lid and press the "STEAM" button. Press the "START/STOP" button; cook for 5 minutes at High pressure.
3. Once cooking is complete, use a natural pressure release and carefully remove the lid. Let cool completely.

Storing

- Divide your jam among sterilized jars, cover with lids, and place in your refrigerator for 10 to 14 days.
- To freeze, spoon your jam into airtight containers. Freeze up to 1 to 2 months. Defrost in the refrigerator.

3. French Toast with Lemon Marmalade and Figs

Try a delicious breakfast recipe made with French bread, eggs, almond milk, and dried figs. You can use Brioche or Fougasse for this recipe.

Servings 4

Ready in about 20 minutes

NUTRITIONAL INFORMATION (Per Serving)

392 - Calories
15.9g - Fat
52.8g - Carbs
12.4g - Protein
29.7g - Sugars

Ingredients

- 8 slices of French bread, cut into pieces
- 3 eggs, beaten
- 3/4 cup almond milk
- 1/4 cup honey
- 1/4 cup lemon marmalade
- 1/2 teaspoon ground cinnamon
- 1/2 teaspoon ground cardamom
- 1/2 teaspoon pure coconut extract
- 1/2 cup dried figs, chopped
- 2 tablespoons butter, melted

Directions

1. Start by adding 1 ½ cups of water and a metal rack to your Crock-Pot Express. Spritz a baking pan with a nonstick cooking spray. Add bread cubes to the pan.
2. In a mixing bowl, thoroughly combine eggs, milk, honey, lemon marmalade, cinnamon, cardamom, and coconut extract.
3. Pour the egg mixture into the baking pan. Top with dried figs and drizzle with melted butter. Lower the pan onto the rack.
4. Secure the lid and press the "DESSERT" button. Press the "START/STOP" button; cook for 15 minutes at High pressure.
5. Once cooking is complete, use a quick pressure release and carefully remove the lid.
6. Let cool completely.

Storing

- Place a sheet of wax paper between each slice of French toast and place them in airtight containers; store in your refrigerator for up 1 to 2 days.
- To freeze, place a sheet of wax paper between each slice of French toast. Wrap them tightly in foil or place in a heavy-duty freezer bag. Use within 1 to 2 months. Bon appétit!

4. Elegant Liver Pâté

Quick cook time and convenience are just a few of the things that make cooking of a classic chicken liver pâté in the Crock-Pot Express so easy!

Servings 8

Ready in about 10 minutes

NUTRITIONAL INFORMATION (Per Serving)

180 - Calories
7.9g - Fat
1.2g - Carbs
23.6g - Protein
0.5g - Sugars

Ingredients

- 3/4 pound chicken livers, trimmed
- 1/2 cup onions, chopped
- 1 teaspoon ginger-garlic paste
- 2/3 cup chicken stock
- 3 tablespoons bourbon
- 2 teaspoons butter, melted
- 1/2 cup heavy cream
- 1 teaspoon dried oregano
- 1/8 teaspoon ground allspice
- Salt and ground black pepper, to taste
- 1/2 teaspoon marjoram
- 2 sage sprigs

Directions

1. Add chicken livers, onions, ginger-garlic paste, chicken stock, bourbon, butter, heavy cream, oregano, allspice, salt, black pepper, and marjoram to your Crock-Pot Express.
2. Secure the lid and press the "STEAM" button. Press the "START/STOP" button; cook for 3 minutes at High pressure.
3. Once cooking is complete, use a quick pressure release and carefully remove the lid.
4. Purée the mixture in a food processor until smooth. Lastly, garnish with sage sprigs. Let cool completely.

Storing

- Spoon your liver pâté into airtight containers; keep in your refrigerator for up to 1 to 2 days.
- For freezing, place your liver pâté in airtight containers or heavy-duty freezer bags. It will maintain the best quality for about 1 to 2 months. Defrost in the refrigerator. Enjoy!

5. Sweet Cornmeal Porridge

Make an ordinary cornmeal mush a little more excessive by adding raisins and chopped walnuts.

Servings 4

Ready in about 15 minutes

NUTRITIONAL INFORMATION (Per Serving)

341 - Calories
10.6g - Fat
50.9g - Carbs
9.9g - Protein
9.3g - Sugars

Ingredients

- 1 cup cornmeal
- 2 cups water
- 2 cups milk
- 1/2 teaspoon ground cinnamon
- 1/2 teaspoon ground cardamom
- 1/2 teaspoon vanilla essence
- 1/4 cup raisins
- 1/4 cup walnuts, finely chopped

Directions

1. Add cornmeal, water, milk, cinnamon, cardamom, and vanilla to the Crock-Pot Express.
2. Secure the lid and press the "RICE/RISOTTO" button. Press the "START/STOP" button; cook for 8 minutes at High pressure.
3. Once cooking is complete, use a natural pressure release and carefully remove the lid.
4. Top with raisins and walnuts. Let cool completely.

Storing

- Spoon the porridge into three airtight containers; keep in your refrigerator for up to 4 days.
- For freezing, scrape the porridge into a food storage container and use it within a few weeks for best results. Defrost in the refrigerator. Enjoy!

6. Scotch Eggs with Ham and Sausage

This recipe uses cooked ham, apple & onion stuffing mix, and ground sausage for a surprisingly delicious breakfast.

Servings 5

Ready in about 20 minutes

NUTRITIONAL INFORMATION (Per Serving)

307 - Calories
21.2g - Fat
1.9g - Carbs
26.3g - Protein
0.6g - Sugars

Ingredients

- 5 eggs
- 3/4 pound ground sausage
- 1/4 pound ham, cooked and shredded
- 1 tablespoon apple & onion stuffing mix
- 1/2 teaspoon thyme, chopped
- 1/2 teaspoon rosemary, chopped
- 1/3 teaspoon sea salt
- 1 teaspoon black peppercorn, crushed
- 2 tablespoons canola oil

Directions

1. Add 1 cup of water and a steamer basket to your Crock-Pot Express. Place the eggs in the steamer basket.
2. Secure the lid and press the "BEANS/CHILI" button. Press the "START/STOP" button; cook for 5 minutes at Low pressure.
3. Once cooking is complete, use a quick pressure release and carefully remove the lid.
4. Transfer the eggs to an ice-cold water in order to cool; peel them and set aside.
5. In a mixing bowl, thoroughly combine ground sausage, ham, apple & onion stuffing mix, thyme, rosemary, salt, and crushed peppercorns.
6. Divide the mixture into five balls; flatten each ball. Place the hard-boiled egg in the center of each ball; now, wrap the sausage mixture around the egg.
7. Press the "BROWN/SAUTÉ" button and set temperature to HIGH. Now, press the "START/STOP" button. Heat the oil and cook the Scotch eggs on all sides.
8. Wipe down the Crock-Pot Express with a damp cloth. Add 1 cup of water and a metal trivet to the bottom of your Crock-Pot Express. Now, place the Scotch eggs on the trivet.
9. Secure the lid and press the "STEAM" button. Press the "START/STOP" button; cook for 5 minutes at High pressure.
10. Once cooking is complete, use a quick pressure release and carefully remove the lid. Let cool completely.

Storing

- Place scotch eggs in two airtight containers or Ziploc bags; keep in the refrigerator for up to 1 week.
- For freezing, divide them between two Ziploc bags; they can be frozen for up to 2 months. Defrost overnight and place in the oven at 175 degrees F for 10 minutes. Bon appétit!

7. Quinoa with Pears and Vanilla

Here's an extravagant and easy breakfast for the whole family! Make sure to use a natural release to prevent the porridge from splattering.

Servings 5

Ready in about 30 minutes

NUTRITIONAL INFORMATION (Per Serving)

440 - Calories
12.1g - Fat
70.7g - Carbs
13.7g - Protein
21.2g - Sugars

Ingredients

- 2 cups quinoa
- 3 cups water
- 2 cups milk
- 1/4 cup Turbinado sugar
- 1 teaspoon vanilla paste
- 1/2 teaspoon cinnamon, ground
- 3 pears, cored and sliced
- 1/2 cup whipped cream

Directions

1. Add all ingredients, except for whipped cream, to your Crock-Pot Express.
2. Secure the lid and press the "MULTIGRAIN" button. Press the "START/STOP" button; cook for 10 minutes at High pressure.
3. Once cooking is complete, use a natural pressure release and carefully remove the lid.
4. Just before serving, top each bowl with whipped cream. Let cool completely.

Storing

- Spoon your quinoa into airtight containers or Ziploc bags; keep in your refrigerator for up to 3 to 5 days.
- For freezing, place your quinoa in airtight containers. Freeze up to 1 month. Defrost in the refrigerator. Bon appétit!

8. Aromatic Sweet Rice

This risotto is cooked to fluffy and creamy perfection in your Crock-Pot Express. You can substitute your favorite jam in place of berry jam.

Servings 5

Ready in about 25 minutes

NUTRITIONAL INFORMATION (Per Serving)

403 - Calories
10.2g - Fat
74.2g - Carbs
5.2g - Protein
36.4g Sugars

Ingredients

- 1 cup white long-grain rice, well-rinsed
- 1 cup coconut milk
- 1/2 cup water
- 1/2 cup coconut cream
- 1/3 cup honey
- A pinch of salt
- A pinch of grated nutmeg
- 1/2 teaspoon pure vanilla essence
- 1/2 teaspoon cardamom, ground
- 1/4 teaspoon star anise, ground
- 1/2 cup berry jam

Directions

1. Add rice, milk, water, coconut cream, honey, salt, nutmeg, vanilla, cardamom, and anise to the Crock-Pot Express.
2. Secure the lid and press the "MULTIGRAIN" button. Press the "START/STOP" button; cook for 20 minutes at High pressure.
3. Once cooking is complete, use a natural pressure release and carefully remove the lid.
4. Lastly, top with berry jam. Let cool completely.

Storing

- Spoon your rice into airtight containers or Ziploc bags; keep in your refrigerator for up to 4 to 6 days.
- For freezing, place your rice in airtight containers. Freeze up to 6 months. Defrost in the refrigerator. Bon appétit!

9. Italian Giant Pancake

A great way to make pancakes for the whole family! You don't have to slave over a hot stove, just turn the Crock-Pot Express on, sit back, and relax.

Servings 4

Ready in about 55 minutes

NUTRITIONAL INFORMATION (Per Serving)

434 - Calories
9.8g - Fat
74.2g - Carbs
13.6g - Protein
37.9g - Sugars

Ingredients

- 3 eggs
- 1 cup milk
- 1/2 cup water
- 1 ½ cups white flour
- 1 teaspoon baking powder
- 1/2 teaspoon kosher salt
- 1 teaspoon brown sugar
- 1 teaspoon grated lemon zest

Directions

1. Whisk the eggs until frothy. Add milk and water; whisk again.
2. Then, add flour, baking powder, salt, brown sugar, and lemon zest. Mix until everything is well combined.
3. Spritz the bottom and sides of your Crock-Pot Express with a nonstick cooking spray. Scrape the batter into the Crock-Pot Express.
4. Secure the lid and press the "MULTIGRAIN" button. Press the "START/STOP" button; cook for 50 minutes at High pressure.
5. Once cooking is complete, use a quick pressure release and carefully remove the lid. Let cool completely.

Storing

- Cover your pancake with foil or plastic wrap to prevent drying out. Keep in your refrigerator for 1 day.
- Wrap the pancake tightly in aluminum foil or place inside a heavy-duty freezer bag and freeze. Use the frozen pancake within 1 to 2 months. Enjoy!

10. Aromatic Oatmeal with Coconut

Want a quick, easy, and nutritious breakfast? A fine, old-fashioned coconut oatmeal is just the thing for you!

Servings 2

Ready in about 15 minutes

NUTRITIONAL INFORMATION (Per Serving)

243 - Calories
11.8g - Fat
48g - Carbs
12.6g - Protein
2.5g - Sugars

Ingredients

- 4 cups water
- 1 ½ cups steel cut oats
- 1 tablespoon coconut oil
- 1/2 teaspoon cardamom
- 1/4 teaspoon grated nutmeg
- 1/2 teaspoon ground cinnamon
- 1/2 teaspoon vanilla essence
- 1/2 teaspoon ground star anise
- 1/2 cup coconut, flaked

Directions

1. Add water and oats to your Crock-Pot Express.
2. Secure the lid and press the "MULTIGRAIN" button. Press the "START/STOP" button; cook for 10 minutes at High pressure.
3. Once cooking is complete, use a quick pressure release and carefully remove the lid.
4. Add coconut oil and seasonings to the warm oatmeal and stir to combine well.

Top with flaked coconut. Let cool completely.

Storing

- Spoon the oatmeal into two airtight containers; keep in your refrigerator for up to 4 to 6 days.
- For freezing, place the oatmeal in airtight containers or heavy-duty freezer bags. It will maintain the best quality for about 6 months. Defrost in the refrigerator. Enjoy!

11. Cilantro Cornbread with Cheese

The perfect mixture of cornmeal, cheese, fresh cilantro, and spices. Salty, sweet, and melty!

Servings 8

Ready in about 35 minutes

NUTRITIONAL INFORMATION (Per Serving)

318 - Calories
14.3g - Fat
37.2g - Carbs
9.9g - Protein
5.6g Sugars

Ingredients

- 1 cup water
- 1 ½ cups cornmeal
- 1/2 cup all-purpose flour
- 1 teaspoon baking soda
- 1 teaspoon baking powder
- 1/2 teaspoon kosher salt
- 1/4 teaspoon black pepper, or more to taste
- 1/4 teaspoon cayenne pepper
- 1/2 teaspoon dried basil
- 1/4 teaspoon dried oregano
- 1/2 teaspoon ground allspice
- 1 cup Pepper-Jack cheese, grated
- 3/4 cup fresh corn kernels
- 2 tablespoons cilantro, roughly chopped
- 1 cup milk
- 1/2 teaspoon lime juice
- 1/2 stick butter, melted
- 2 tablespoons pure maple syrup
- 2 eggs

Directions

1. Add water and a metal trivet to the base of your Crock-Pot Express. Lightly grease a baking pan that fits in your Crock-Pot Express.
2. In a mixing bowl, thoroughly combine the cornmeal, flour, baking soda, baking powder, salt, black pepper, cayenne pepper, basil, oregano, and allspice.
3. Stir in Pepper-Jack cheese, corn kernels, and cilantro. Mix to combine well.
4. In another mixing bowl, whisk the remaining ingredients; add this wet mixture to the dry mixture.
5. Pour the batter into the prepared baking pan. Cover with a paper towel; then, top with foil.
6. Lower the pan onto the trivet and secure the lid.
7. Secure the lid and press the "RICE/RISOTTO" button. Press the "START/STOP" button; cook for 25 minutes at High pressure.
8. Once cooking is complete, use a natural pressure release and carefully remove the lid. Transfer to a wire rack to sit for 5 to 10 minutes.

Storing

- Place your cornbread in a breadbox or wrap in foil; store for about 1 to 2 days at room temperature.
- Place in a storage bag and transfer to your refrigerator; it will last for 1 week before getting stale.
- For freezing, wrap the loaf with clear plastic bread bags. Freeze up to 2 to 3 months. To thaw the frozen cornbread, let it come to room temperature.
- Just before serving, place your cornbread in an oven heated to 400 degrees F for about 4 minutes.

12. Corn Muffins with Coleslaw

Combine your favorites into one great bite! Cheese, butter and eggs combine well in these cornbread muffins that are served with famous coleslaw.

Servings 6

Ready in about 25 minutes

NUTRITIONAL INFORMATION (Per Serving)

410 - Calories
20.7g - Fat
43.2g - Carbs
12.1g - Protein
7.5g - Sugars

Ingredients

- 1/2 cup all-purpose flour
- 1 1/3 cups yellow cornmeal
- 1 teaspoon baking powder
- 1 teaspoon baking soda
- 1 teaspoon sugar
- 1 teaspoon salt
- 1 cup milk
- 1/2 stick butter, melted
- 1 egg
- 1 cup Monterey-Jack cheese, shredded
- 1 cup prepared coleslaw

Directions

1. Mix the flour, baking powder, baking soda, sugar, and salt in a bowl. In a separate bowl, whisk the milk, butter, and eggs.
2. Add the wet mixture to the dry mixture. Fold in shredded cheese; mix again. Scrape the batter into a baking pan.
3. Add 1 cup of water and a metal trivet to the bottom of your Crock-Pot Express. Then, lower the baking pan onto the trivet.
4. Secure the lid and press the "MULTIGRAIN" button. Press the "START/STOP" button; cook for 20 minutes at High pressure.
5. Once cooking is complete, use a natural pressure release and carefully remove the lid.
6. Transfer to a cooling rack before unmolding.

Storing

- Wrap corn muffins in foil; store for about 1 to 2 days at room temperature.
- Place in a storage bag and transfer to your refrigerator; corn muffins will last for 1 week before getting stale.
- Place prepared coleslaw in airtight containers; it will last for 3 to 5 days in the refrigerator.
- For freezing, wrap corn muffins with clear plastic bread bags. Freeze up to 2 to 3 months. To thaw the frozen corn muffin, let it come to room temperature.

13. Breakfast Cupcakes with Fresh Apricots

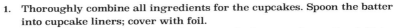

These are the best apricot cupcakes you've ever had! With a gorgeous almond butter frosting, they are perfect for any occasion!

Servings 6

Ready in about 30 minutes

NUTRITIONAL INFORMATION (Per Serving)

311 - Calories
13.9g - Fat
46.5g - Carbs
4.3g - Protein
44.2g - Sugars

Ingredients

Cupcakes:
- 1 cup apricots, pitted and chopped
- 3/4 cup almond flour
- 1 teaspoon baking powder
- A pinch of coarse salt
- 2 eggs, beaten
- 1/2 teaspoon vanilla paste
- 1/2 cup honey
- 1/4 almond milk

Frosting:
- 1/3 cup almond butter
- 1 teaspoon cocoa powder
- 3 tablespoons honey

Directions

1. Thoroughly combine all ingredients for the cupcakes. Spoon the batter into cupcake liners; cover with foil.
2. Add 1 cup of water and a metal trivet to the bottom of your Crock-Pot Express. Now, place the cupcake liners on the trivet.
3. Secure the lid and press the "RICE/RISOTTO" button. Press the "START/STOP" button; cook for 25 minutes at High pressure.
4. Once cooking is complete, use a natural pressure release and carefully remove the lid.
5. Meanwhile, prepare the frosting by mixing all ingredients. Transfer to a plastic bag for piping the frosting on your cupcakes. Let cool completely.

Storing

- Place cupcakes in airtight containers or cover with foil or plastic wrap to prevent drying out; your cupcakes will last for about 1 to 2 days at room temperature.
- Place your cupcakes in the airtight containers or Ziploc bags; keep in the refrigerator for a week.
- For freezing, wrap cupcakes tightly with aluminum foil or plastic freezer wrap, or place in heavy-duty freezer bag; freeze up to 4 to 6 months. Defrost in your microwave for a couple of minutes. Bon appétit!

14. Pineapple Compote with Dried Fruits

Save this recipe as a lovely addition to your special brunch.
Feel free to experiment with this recipe and add your
favorite combo of fruits.

Servings 8

Ready in about
15 minutes

NUTRITIONAL
INFORMATION
(Per Serving)

276 - Calories
11.6g - Fat
45g - Carbs
1.2g - Protein
42.2g - Sugars

Ingredients

- 1/2 cup granulated sugar
- 1 stick butter, at room temperature
- 1/4 teaspoon ground nutmeg
- 1/2 teaspoon ground cinnamon
- 20 ounces peaches, pitted and sliced
- 10 ounces canned pineapple
- 2 cups water
- 1 cup pineapple juice
- 1/3 cup dried raisins, chopped
- 1/3 cup dried figs, chopped

Directions

1. Add all of the above ingredients to your Crock-Pot Express.
2. Secure the lid and press the "STEAM" button. Press the "START/STOP" button; cook for 8 minutes at High pressure.
3. Once cooking is complete, use a natural pressure release and carefully remove the lid. Let cool completely.

Storing

- Spoon your compote into covered glass or plastic container. Refrigerate for 5 to 7 days.
- To freeze, place your compote in airtight containers or heavy-duty freezer bags. It will maintain the best quality for about 2 months. Bon appétit!

15. Chocolate and Coconut Nalesniki

Nalesniki are Polish crepes. Serve with jam, fresh or dried fruits, and other toppings.

Servings 4

Ready in about 55 minutes

NUTRITIONAL INFORMATION (Per Serving)

302 - Calories
7.4g - Fat
46.5g - Carbs
11.5g - Protein
10g - Sugars

Ingredients

- 1 ½ cups flour
- 1 teaspoon baking powder
- 1 teaspoon baking powder
- 1 cup coconut milk
- 2 eggs, whisked
- 1/4 cup granulated sugar
- 2 teaspoons cocoa powder
- 1/4 cup coconut, shredded
- A pinch of salt
- A pinch of grated nutmeg

Directions

1. Mix the ingredients until everything is well incorporated.
2. Spritz the inside of your Crock-Pot Express with a nonstick cooking spray.
3. Scrape the batter into the Crock-Pot Express.
4. Secure the lid and press the "MULTIGRAIN" button. Press the "START/STOP" button; cook for 50 minutes at High pressure.
5. Once cooking is complete, use a quick pressure release and carefully remove the lid. Let cool completely.

Storing

- Cover your crepe with foil or plastic wrap to prevent drying out. Keep in your refrigerator for 1 day.
- Wrap the crepe tightly in aluminum foil or place inside a heavy-duty freezer bag and freeze. Use the frozen pancake within 1 to 2 months. Enjoy!

16. Bread Pudding with Bacon and Cheese

Undoubtedly, this is a very versatile recipe. A fancy bread pudding is much simpler to prepare than you might expect!

Servings 6

Ready in about 40 minutes

NUTRITIONAL INFORMATION (Per Serving)

385 - Calories
25.3g - Fat
17.1g - Carbs
21.8g - Protein
4.1g - Sugars

Ingredients

- 1 loaf of sourdough bread, cut into chunks
- 2 tablespoons butter, melted
- 6 slices Canadian bacon, chopped
- 6 ounces Monterey-Jack cheese, grated
- 3 eggs, beaten
- 1/2 cup milk
- 1/2 cup cream cheese
- 1/4 teaspoon marjoram
- 1 teaspoon onion powder
- Garlic salt and ground black pepper, to taste

Directions

1. Prepare your Crock-Pot Express by adding 1 ½ cups of water and a metal rack to its bottom.
2. Spritz the bottom and sides of a soufflé dish with a nonstick cooking spray. Add 1/2 of bread cubes to the bottom of the dish; drizzle the melted butter over them.
3. Add bacon and grated Monterey-Jack cheese. Add the remaining 1/2 of bread cubes.
4. In a mixing bowl, thoroughly combine the eggs, milk, cheese marjoram, onion powder, garlic salt, and black pepper. Pour this mixture over the top.
5. Lower the soufflé dish onto the prepared metal rack. Cover with a piece of foil.
6. Secure the lid and press the "BEANS/CHILI" button. Press the "START/ STOP" button; cook for 20 minutes at Low pressure.
7. Once cooking is complete, use a quick pressure release and carefully remove the lid.
8. Allow it to stand on a cooling rack for 10 to 15 minutes. Let cool completely.

Storing

- Spoon bread pudding into airtight containers; keep in your refrigerator for up to 5 to 6 days.
- For freezing, place bread pudding in airtight containers or heavy-duty freezer bags. It will maintain the best quality for about 2 to 3 months. Defrost in your refrigerator. Bon appétit!

17. Buckwheat with Tuna and Peppers

This salad is so fresh and healthy! Simply combine farmer's market veggies, fresh-from-the-sea tuna, and extra-virgin olive oil and dig in!

Servings 4

Ready in about 10 minutes + chilling time

NUTRITIONAL INFORMATION (Per Serving)

238 - Calories
6.8g - Fat
14.1g - Carbs
30.1g - Protein
3.3g - Sugars

Ingredients

- 1 pound tuna, cut into bite-sized pieces
- 1 cup buckwheat
- 1/2 teaspoon dried or fresh dill
- Salt and black pepper, to taste
- 2 cups water
- 1 white onion, thinly sliced
- 2 bell peppers, seeded and thinly sliced
- 1 carrot, grated
- 1 large-sized cucumber, thinly sliced
- 1/4 cup extra-virgin olive oil
- 2 tablespoons lemon juice, freshly squeezed

Directions

1. Throw the water, buckwheat, dill, salt, black pepper, and water into your Crock-Pot Express.
2. Secure the lid and press the "STEAM" button. Press the "START/STOP" button; cook for 3 minutes at Low pressure.
3. Once cooking is complete, use a quick pressure release and carefully remove the lid. Then, toss it with the remaining ingredients. Let cool completely.

Storing

- Spoon your salad into airtight containers or Ziploc bags; keep in your refrigerator for up to 3 to 5 days.
- For freezing, place your salad in airtight containers. Freeze up to 1 month. Defrost in the refrigerator. Bon appétit!

18. Polenta with Cremini Mushrooms and Olives

If you don't think you like polenta, try this recipe! Polenta, vegetables, and feta cheese are healthy and full of delicious flavors.

Servings 3

Ready in about 15 minutes

NUTRITIONAL INFORMATION (Per Serving)

420 - Calories
26.2g - Fat
32.1g - Carbs
17.8g - Protein
6.3g - Sugars

Ingredients

- 2 tablespoons butter, at room temperature
- 1 cup scallions, chopped
- 2 garlic cloves, smashed
- 1 pound Crimini mushrooms, thinly sliced
- 1/2 teaspoon dried oregano
- 1/2 teaspoon dried basil
- 1/2 teaspoon dried dill weed
- Sea salt and freshly ground black pepper, to taste
- 1 teaspoon cayenne pepper
- 2 cups water
- 2 cups vegetable broth
- 1 cup polenta
- 1 cup Kalamata olives, pitted and sliced
- 6 ounces feta cheese, crumbled

Directions

1. Press the "BROWN/SAUTÉ" button and set temperature to HIGH; press the "START/STOP" button. Now, melt the butter and cook the scallions until tender.
2. Stir in the garlic and mushrooms; cook an additional 40 seconds or until aromatic.
3. Then, add herbs, salt, black pepper, and cayenne pepper. Add a splash of water to deglaze the pot; reserve the mushroom mixture. Press the "START/STOP" button. Add the water and broth. Press the "BROWN/SAUTÉ" button and set temperature to HIGH; press the "START/STOP" button. Slowly and gradually, pour the polenta into the liquid; make sure to whisk continuously.
4. Secure the lid and press the "BEANS/CHILI" button. Press the "START/STOP" button; cook for 5 minutes at High pressure.
5. Once cooking is complete, use a quick pressure release and carefully remove the lid.
6. Top warm polenta with mushroom mixture, olives, and feta cheese. Let cool completely.

Storing

- Spoon the polenta into three airtight containers; keep in your refrigerator for up to 4 days.
- For freezing, scrape the polenta into a food storage container and use frozen polenta within 2 weeks for the best results. Defrost in the refrigerator. Enjoy!

19. Oriental-Style Oatmeal

Are you looking for a no-fuss family breakfast? This sweet
and flavorful oatmeal is ready in 15 minutes!

Servings 4

**Ready in about
15 minutes**

**NUTRITIONAL
INFORMATION
(Per Serving)**

347 - Calories
12.1g - Fat
51.3g - Carbs
8.7g - Protein
25.1g - Sugars

Ingredients

- 1 ½ cups regular oats
- 2 cups water
- 2 cups almond milk
- 1 teaspoon cinnamon, ground
- 2 tablespoons almond butter
- 1/2 cup chocolate chips

Directions

1. Simply throw the oats, water, milk, and cinnamon into
   the Crock-Pot Express.
2. Secure the lid and press the "MULTIGRAIN" button.
   Press the "START/STOP" button; cook for 10 minutes at
   High pressure.
3. Once cooking is complete, use a quick pressure release
   and carefully remove the lid. Let cool completely. Top
   with almond butter and chocolate chips.

Storing

- Spoon the oatmeal into airtight containers; keep in
  your refrigerator for up to 4 to 6 days.
- For freezing, place the oatmeal in airtight containers
  or heavy-duty freezer bags. It will maintain the best
  quality for about 6 months. Defrost in the refrigerator.
  Enjoy!

20. Upma with Mushrooms and Peppers

If you like a super creamy oatmeal, keep this recipe in your back pocket. Indian spices, cream of mushroom soup and bell pepper will add something special to your regular oats.

Servings 4

Ready in about 10 minutes

NUTRITIONAL INFORMATION (Per Serving)

384 - Calories
12.3g - Fat
75.1g - Carbs
12.8g - Protein
3.6g - Sugars

Ingredients

- 1 tablespoon ghee
- 1 small-sized leek, finely diced
- 1 teaspoon garlic, minced
- 1/2 pound button mushrooms, chopped
- 1 red bell pepper, chopped
- 1 ¼ cups oat bran
- 2 cups water
- 2 cups cream of mushroom soup
- 1 sprig curry leaves
- 1/2 teaspoon chana dal
- 1/2 teaspoon urad dal
- 1/4 teaspoon ground turmeric
- 1/4 teaspoon dried dill
- Sea salt and ground black pepper, to taste

Directions

1. Press the "BROWN/SAUTÉ" button and set temperature to HIGH; press the "START/STOP" button. Now, melt the ghee and cook the leek until tender and fragrant.
2. Then, stir in the garlic, mushrooms and pepper; cook an additional 2 minutes; reserve.
3. Wipe down the Crock-Pot Express with a damp cloth. Stir the remaining ingredients into your Crock-Pot Express.
4. Secure the lid and press the "STEAM" button. Press the "START/STOP" button; cook for 3 minutes at High pressure.
5. Once cooking is complete, use a natural pressure release and carefully remove the lid.
6. Top with the reserved mushroom mixture. Let cool completely.

Storing

- Spoon the oatmeal into airtight containers; keep in your refrigerator for up to 4 to 6 days.
- For freezing, place the oatmeal in airtight containers or heavy-duty freezer bags. It will maintain the best quality for about 6 months. Defrost in the refrigerator.

LUNCH

21. Traditional Onion Soup

Every home cook needs a homemade chicken stock. Make your stock today and keep it in your refrigerator for up to 4 days.

Servings 6

Ready in about 25 minutes

NUTRITIONAL INFORMATION (Per Serving)

353 - Calories
15.4g - Fat
40.5g - Carbs
15.4g - Protein
20.2g - Sugars

Ingredients

- 3 tablespoons ghee
- 6 sweet onions, sliced
- 2 garlic cloves
- Kosher salt and ground black pepper, to taste
- 1/2 teaspoon cayenne pepper
- 1 tablespoon granulated sugar
- 1/3 cup sherry wine
- 1/2 cup water
- 5 cups chicken stock, preferably homemade
- 2 fresh rosemary sprigs
- 1 loaf French bread, cut into slices and toasted
- 1 ½ cups Munster cheese, shaved

Directions

1. Press the "BROWN/SAUTÉ" button and set temperature to HIGH; press the "START/STOP" button. Then, melt the ghee; sauté the onions until translucent, about 5 minutes.
2. Add garlic and sauté it for 1 to 2 minutes more. Next, add the salt, black pepper, cayenne pepper, and white sugar. Continue to cook, stirring frequently, until sweet onions are slightly browned.
3. Pour in sherry wine, and scrape off any brown bits from the bottom of your Crock-Pot Express. Now, pour in the water and chicken stock; add rosemary and stir to combine.
4. Secure the lid and press the "SOUP" button. Press the "START/STOP" button; cook for 8 minutes at High pressure.
5. Once cooking is complete, use a quick pressure release and carefully remove the lid. Then, preheat your oven to broil.
6. Top with toasted bread and shaved Munster cheese; place your soup under the broiler for 5 to 6 minutes or until the cheese is bubbly. Let cool completely.

Storing

- Spoon the soup into airtight containers; keep in your refrigerator for up to 4 days.
- For freezing, place the soup in airtight containers or heavy-duty freezer bags. Freeze up to 4 months.
- Defrost in the microwave or refrigerator. Bon appétit!

22. Family Winter Soup

This family soup features root veggies cooked with high-quality aromatics. The Crock-Pot Express turns dull vegetables into something magnificent!

Servings 8

Ready in about 45 minutes

NUTRITIONAL INFORMATION (Per Serving)

150 - Calories
6.7g - Fat
18.9g - Carbs
4.7g - Protein
3.3g - Sugars

Ingredients

- 2 stalks celery, chopped
- 2 parsnips, chopped
- 2 carrots, chopped
- 1 pound potatoes, cubed
- 1/2 pound turnip, chopped
- 1 onion, chopped
- 2 garlic cloves, minced
- 4 cups water, or as needed
- 3 cups chicken stock
- 1/2 stick butter, at room temperature
- 1/2 teaspoon mustard seeds
- 2 bay leaves
- 1 teaspoon paprika
- 1/2 teaspoon ground black pepper
- Salt, to taste

Directions

1. Place the celery, parsnip, carrots, potatoes, turnip, onion and garlic in the Crock-Pot Express; now, pour in the water and stock.
2. Secure the lid and press the "SOUP" button. Press the "START/STOP" button; cook for 25 minutes at High pressure.
3. Once cooking is complete, use a quick pressure release and carefully remove the lid.
4. Stir in the butter and seasonings. Press the "BROWN/SAUTÉ" button and continue to cook the soup for 14 to 16 minutes more or until everything is heated through. Discard bay leaves.
5. Let cool completely.

Storing

- Spoon your soup into four airtight containers; keep in your refrigerator for up to 4 days.
- For freezing, place your soup in airtight containers or heavy-duty freezer bags. Freeze up to 4 months.
- Defrost in the refrigerator or microwave.

23. Mom's Creamy Chowder

This good-for-you chowder is loaded with vegetables, dairy and simple seasonings. Moreover, it is a cinch to make in the Crock-Pot Express.

Servings 6

Ready in about 35 minutes

NUTRITIONAL INFORMATION (Per Serving)

193 - Calories
5.5g - Fat
28.6g - Carbs
9.2g - Protein
2.1g - Sugars

Ingredients

- 1/2 cup leeks, chopped
- 1 pound broccoli, broken into small florets
- 1/2 pound celery, chopped
- 1 carrot, sliced
- 2 potatoes, peeled and diced
- 3 cups water
- 2 cups roasted-vegetable stock
- Kosher salt, to taste
- 1/4 teaspoon ground black pepper
- 1/4 teaspoon red pepper flakes, crushed
- 1 cup sour cream

Directions

1. Simply place all of the above ingredients, except for sour cream, in your Crock-Pot Express.
2. Secure the lid and press the "SOUP" button. Press the "START/STOP" button; cook for 30 minutes at High pressure.
3. Once cooking is complete, use a quick pressure release and carefully remove the lid.
4. Then, puree the soup with an immersion blender; add sour cream. Let cool completely.

Storing

- Spoon your chowder into airtight containers; keep in your refrigerator for up to 4 days.
- For freezing, place your chowder in heavy-duty freezer bags. When the bags are frozen through, stack them up like file folders to save space in the freezer.
- Freeze up to 4 months. Defrost in the microwave or refrigerator. Bon appétit!

24. The Best Vegetarian Stroganoff Ever

Are you looking for a classic family lunch? This recipe will fit the bill. You can use Italian or crimini mushroom in this recipe.

Servings 8

Ready in about 45 minutes

NUTRITIONAL INFORMATION (Per Serving)

137 - Calories
3.9g - Fat
23g - Carbs
4.5g - Protein
2.8g - Sugars

Ingredients

- 2 tablespoons olive oil
- 1 cup shallots, chopped
- 2 garlic cloves, minced
- 2 russet potatoes, chopped
- 1 celery with leaves, chopped
- 1 bell pepper, seeded and thinly sliced
- 1 habanero pepper, minced
- 14 ounces brown mushrooms, thinly sliced
- 1 cup water
- 1 cup vegetable stock
- Sea salt and ground black pepper, to taste
- 1/2 teaspoon Hungarian paprika
- 1/2 teaspoon cayenne pepper
- 2 bay leaves
- 1 ripe tomato, seeded and chopped
- 2 tablespoons corn flour, plus 3 tablespoons of water

Directions

1. Press the "BROWN/SAUTÉ" button and set temperature to HIGH; press the "START/STOP" button.
2. Then, heat the olive oil and sauté the shallot, garlic, potatoes, and celery until they are softened; add a splash of vegetable stock, if needed.
3. Stir in the mushrooms, water, stock, paprika, cayenne pepper, bay leaves, and tomatoes.
4. Secure the lid and press the "MEAT/STEW" button. Press the "START/STOP" button; cook for 35 minutes at High pressure.
5. Once cooking is complete, use a quick pressure release and carefully remove the lid.
6. Make the slurry by whisking the corn flour with 3 tablespoons of water. Add the slurry back to the Crock-Pot Express and press the "BROWN/ SAUTÉ" button one more time.
7. Allow it to cook until the liquid has thickened. Discard bay leaves. Let cool completely.

Storing

- Spoon the stew into airtight containers or Ziploc bags; keep in your refrigerator for up to 3 to 4 days.
- For freezing, place the stew in airtight containers. Freeze up to 4 to 6 months. Defrost in the refrigerator. Bon appétit!

25. Chowder with Cauliflower and Sausage

This rich chowder calls for chicken sausage, cauliflower and spinach. Serve with garlic croutons or a toasted cheese sandwich for a complete meal.

Servings 8

Ready in about 15 minutes

NUTRITIONAL INFORMATION (Per Serving)

360 - Calories
28.1g - Fat
7.8g - Carbs
19.1g - Protein
2.7g - Sugar

Ingredients

- 1 tablespoon lard, melted
- 8 ounces chicken sausage, cooked and thinly sliced
- 1/2 cup scallions, chopped
- 1 teaspoon ginger garlic paste
- 1 pound cauliflower, chopped into florets
- 4 cups vegetable broth
- 1 pinch red pepper flakes
- Kosher salt, to taste
- 1/2 teaspoon freshly ground black pepper, to taste
- 1 cup spinach, torn into pieces

Directions

1. Add all ingredients, except for spinach, to your Crock-Pot Express.
2. Secure the lid and press the "SOUP" button. Press the "START/STOP" button; cook for 9 minutes at High pressure.
3. Once cooking is complete, use a quick pressure release and carefully remove the lid. Puree the mixture in your food processor.
4. Afterwards, add spinach and seal the lid. Let it stand until the spinach is wilted. Let cool completely.

Storing

- Spoon your chowder into airtight containers; keep in your refrigerator for up to 4 days.
- For freezing, place your chowder in heavy-duty freezer bags. When the bags are frozen through, stack them up like file folders to save space in the freezer.
- Freeze up to 4 months. Defrost in the microwave or refrigerator. Bon appétit!

26. Hearty Chicken Soup

Two words: Chicken Soup. This recipe might become your go-to!

Servings 4

Ready in about 25 minutes

NUTRITIONAL INFORMATION (Per Serving)

263 - Calories
9.9g - Fat
15.2g - Carbs
27.7g - Protein
3.3g - Sugars

Ingredients

- 1 ½ tablespoons butter, softened
- 1 cup leeks, thinly sliced
- Sea salt and freshly ground black pepper, to taste
- 1 pound chicken wings, halved
- 2 carrots, chopped
- 1 celery with leaves, chopped
- 2 garlic cloves, finely minced
- 3 cups water
- 1 tablespoon chicken granulated bouillon
- 1 tablespoon flaxseed meal
- 1 tablespoon champagne vinegar

Directions

1. Press the "BROWN/SAUTÉ" button and set temperature to HIGH; press the "START/STOP" button. Now, melt the butter; sauté the leeks until just tender and fragrant.
2. Now, add the salt, pepper, chicken, carrots, celery, and garlic. Continue to sauté until the chicken is no longer pink and the vegetables are softened.
3. Add a splash of water to prevent burning and sticking.
4. Secure the lid and press the "SOUP" button. Press the "START/STOP" button; cook for 20 minutes at High pressure.
5. Once cooking is complete, use a quick pressure release and carefully remove the lid.
6. Then, press the "BROWN/SAUTÉ" button again. Make the slurry by whisking flaxseed meal with a few tablespoons of the cooking liquid. Return the slurry to the Crock-Pot Express and stir to combine.
7. Add champagne vinegar and cook for 1 to 2 minutes more. Let cool completely.

Storing

- Spoon your soup into four airtight containers; keep in your refrigerator for up to 4 days.
- For freezing, place your soup in airtight containers or heavy-duty freezer bags. Freeze up to 4 months.
- Defrost in the refrigerator or microwave. Bon appétit!

27. Traditional Paprikash with Root Vegetables

Traditional Hungarian Paprikash will please the whole family. The turkey legs, vegetables, and seasonings all cook in the Crock-Pot Express for a memorable flavor. The recipe is generous with meat and root veggies for your well-balanced diet.

Servings 4

Ready in about 25 minutes

NUTRITIONAL INFORMATION (Per Serving)

403 - Calories
18.5g - Fat
17.1g - Carbs
40.9g - Protein
6g - Sugars

Ingredients

- 2 tablespoons butter, at room temperature
- 1 pound turkey legs
- Sea salt and ground black pepper, to taste
- 2 cups turkey stock
- 1/2 cup leeks, chopped
- 2 garlic cloves, minced
- 1 red bell pepper, chopped
- 1 green bell pepper, chopped
- 1 Serrano pepper, chopped
- 1 parsnip, chopped
- 1 cup turnip, chopped
- 1/2 pound carrots, chopped
- 2 tablespoons fresh cilantro leaves, chopped
- 1/2 teaspoon Hungarian paprika

Directions

1. Press the "BROWN/SAUTÉ" button and set temperature to HIGH; press the "START/STOP" button; melt the butter. Now, sear the turkey, skin side down, 3 minutes on each side.
2. Sprinkle turkey legs with salt and black pepper as you cook them.
3. Stir the remaining ingredients into the Crock-Pot Express.
4. Secure the lid and press the "MEAT/STEW" button. Press the "START/ STOP" button; cook for 20 minutes at High pressure.
5. Once cooking is complete, use a natural pressure release and carefully remove the lid.
6. Transfer the turkey legs to a bowl and let them cool. Then, strip the meat off the bones, cut it into small pieces and return to the Crock-Pot Express.
7. Let cool completely.

Storing

- Spoon your paprikash into airtight containers or Ziploc bags; keep in your refrigerator for up to 3 to 4 days.
- For freezing, place your paprikash in airtight containers. Freeze up to 4 to 6 months. Defrost in the refrigerator. Bon appétit!

28. Beef Stew with Crispy Topper

Enjoy delicious one-pot meals! Muffin-topped stew is the perfect family dinner, both easy and gourmet!

Servings 8

Ready in about 45 minutes

NUTRITIONAL INFORMATION (Per Serving)

404 - Calories
15.5g - Fat
31.1g - Carbs
34.4g - Protein
7g - Sugars

Ingredients

- 1 heaping tablespoon lard, at room temperature
- 1 ½ pounds beef steak, thinly sliced
- 1 large-sized leek, chopped
- 2 garlic cloves, crushed
- 1 cup celery with leaves
- 1 cup carrots, chopped
- 1 cup parsnip, chopped
- 2 bell peppers, chopped
- 1 (14-ounce) can tomatoes, diced
- 4 cups water
- 4 bouillon cubes
- 1 bay leaf

Topping:
- 1 cup plain flour
- 1 teaspoon baking powder
- 1 cup Swiss cheese, grated
- 1/2 cup full-fat milk

Directions

1. Press the "BROWN/SAUTÉ" button and set temperature to HIGH; press the "START/STOP" button. Melt the lard and brown the beef for 3 to 4 minutes, stirring occasionally.
2. Then, add the leeks and cook an additional 2 minutes or until it has softened. Add the garlic, celery, carrot, parsnip, peppers, tomatoes, water, bouillon cubes, and bay leaf.
3. Secure the lid and press the "MEAT/STEW" button. Press the "START/STOP" button; cook for 20 minutes at High pressure.
4. Once cooking is complete, use a natural pressure release and carefully remove the lid.
5. In a mixing bowl, thoroughly combine all of the topping ingredients. Spread the topping over the top of your stew. Seal the lid and press the "BROWN/SAUTÉ" button.
6. Let it simmer for 15 minutes longer or until golden. Let cool completely.

Storing

- Spoon the stew into airtight containers or Ziploc bags; keep in your refrigerator for up to 3 to 4 days.
- For freezing, place the stew in airtight containers. Freeze up to 4 to 6 months. Defrost in the refrigerator. Bon appétit!

29. The Best Bolognese Ever

In a rush? Don't worry, you can have an amazing family meal in 30 minutes.

Servings 4

Ready in about 30 minutes

NUTRITIONAL INFORMATION (Per Serving)

677 - Calories
39.5g - Fat
37.9g - Carbs
43.3g - Protein
2.5g - Sugars

Ingredients

- 1 ½ tablespoons olive oil
- 1 cup leeks, chopped
- 2 garlic cloves, minced
- 1 pound ground pork
- 1/2 pound ground beef
- 1 celery stick, diced small
- 1 sweet pepper, finely chopped
- 1 jalapeno, finely chopped
- 1 ½ cups broth, preferably homemade
- 1 (28-ounce) can Italian tomatoes, finely chopped
- 2 pounds penne rigate
- 1/4 cup heavy cream

Directions

1. Press the "BROWN/SAUTÉ" button and set temperature to HIGH; press the "START/STOP" button; add the oil. Once hot, sweat the leeks for 3 to 4 minutes, stirring frequently.
2. Add the garlic and cook for 30 seconds more. Add ground meat and cook for 3 minutes more or until it is just browned.
3. Secure the lid and press the "MEAT/STEW" button. Press the "START/STOP" button; cook for 15 minutes at High pressure.
4. Once cooking is complete, use a quick pressure release and carefully remove the lid.
5. Press the "BROWN/SAUTÉ" button and fold in heavy cream; stir until heated through.
6. Let cool completely.

Storing

- Spoon your Bolognese into airtight containers or Ziploc bags; keep in your refrigerator for up to 3 to 4 days.
- For freezing, place your Bolognese in airtight containers. Freeze up to 4 to 6 months. Defrost in the refrigerator. Bon appétit!

30. Easy Hamburger Soup

This hearty and meaty soup is a perfect idea on cold autumn days. Serve with enough crusty, sauce-sopping bread.

Servings 4

Ready in about 25 minutes

NUTRITIONAL INFORMATION (Per Serving)

340 - Calories
16.3g - Fat
15.7g - Carbs
31.9g - Protein
7.2g - Sugars

Ingredients

- 1 tablespoon olive oil
- 1 pound ground beef
- 1 onion, peeled and finely chopped
- Sea salt and ground black pepper, to taste
- 1 teaspoon cayenne pepper
- 1 parsnip, thinly sliced
- 2 carrots, thinly sliced
- 4 cups beef bone broth
- 2 garlic cloves, minced
- 1/2 cup tomato purée

Directions

1. Press the "BROWN/SAUTÉ" button and set temperature to HIGH; press the "START/STOP" button. Heat the olive oil and brown the ground beef and onions until the meat is no longer pink.
2. Add the remaining ingredients to your Crock-Pot Express.
3. Secure the lid and press the "SOUP" button. Press the "START/STOP" button; cook for 20 minutes at High pressure.
4. Once cooking is complete, use a quick pressure release and carefully remove the lid. Let cool completely.

Storing

- Spoon your soup into airtight containers; keep in your refrigerator for up to 4 days.
- For freezing, place your soup in heavy-duty freezer bags. When the bags are frozen through, stack them up like file folders to save space in the freezer.
- Freeze up to 4 months. Defrost in the microwave or refrigerator. Bon appétit!

31. Traditional Beef Pepperonata

If you like beef and bell peppers, you should try this Italian classic. Serve on Semelle rolls just like Italian nonna used to make.

Servings 6

Ready in about 1 hour 10 minutes

NUTRITIONAL INFORMATION (Per Serving)

309 - Calories
7.4g - Fat
10.8g - Carbs
46.9g - Protein
5.1g - Sugars

Ingredients

- 2 teaspoons lard, at room temperature
- 2 pounds top round steak, cut into bite-sized chunks
- 1 red onion, chopped
- 1 pound mixed bell peppers, deveined and thinly sliced
- 2 cloves garlic, minced
- 1 tablespoon Italian seasoning blend
- Sea salt and ground black pepper, to taste
- 1 tablespoon salt-packed capers, rinsed and drained
- 1/2 cup dry red wine
- 1 cup water

Directions

1. Press the "BROWN/SAUTÉ" button and set temperature to HIGH; press the "START/STOP" button. Then, melt the lard. Cook the round steak approximately 5 minutes, stirring periodically; reserve.
2. Then, sauté the onion for 2 minutes or until translucent.
3. Stir in the remaining ingredients, including the reserved beef.
4. Secure the lid and press the "MEAT/STEW" button. Press the "START/STOP" button; cook for 60 minutes at High pressure.
5. Once cooking is complete, use a natural pressure release and carefully remove the lid. Let cool completely.

Storing

- Place beef Pepperonata in airtight containers or Ziploc bags; keep in your refrigerator for up to 3 to 4 days.
- For freezing, place beef Pepperonata in airtight containers or heavy-duty freezer bags. Freeze up to 2 to 3 months. Defrost in the refrigerator. Bon appétit!

32. Paprika Seafood Jambalaya

Smoked sausage, fish, and paprika make a great blend.
Serve with a horseradish sauce if desired.

Servings 4

**Ready in about
10 minutes**

**NUTRITIONAL
INFORMATION
(Per Serving)**

301 - Calories
14.8g - Fat
10.1g - Carbs
31.4g - Protein
3.9g - Sugars

Ingredients

- 2 cups chicken stock
- 8 ounces smoked sausage, cut into bite-sized pieces
- 1 pound catfish
- 1 celery with leaves, chopped
- 1 carrot, chopped
- 1 leek, thinly sliced
- 2 garlic cloves, minced
- Sea salt and ground black pepper, to taste
- 1 teaspoon smoked paprika
- 1 teaspoon hot paprika
- 1 teaspoon Old Bay seasoning
- 2 tomatoes, chopped

Directions

1. Add all of the above ingredients to your Crock-Pot Express.
2. Secure the lid and press the "SOUP" button. Press the "START/STOP" button; cook for 5 minutes at High pressure.
3. Once cooking is complete, use a quick pressure release and carefully remove the lid.
4. Remove all ingredients from the Crock-Pot Express using a slotted spoon. Let cool completely.

Storing

- Spoon Jambalaya into airtight containers; it will last for 3 to 4 days in the refrigerator.
- For freezing, place Jambalaya in airtight containers or heavy-duty freezer bags. Freeze up to 4 to 6 months. Defrost in the microwave or refrigerator. Bon appétit!

33. Family Bean Soup

Thanks to the Crock-Pot Express, making a homemade bean soup is easier than you ever thought. You will go one step further with this recipe and make a hearty family soup in less than 40 minutes.

Servings 5

Ready in about 35 minutes

NUTRITIONAL INFORMATION (Per Serving)

188 - Calories
9.6g - Fat
16.2g - Carbs
11.9g - Protein
4g - Sugars

Ingredients

- 2 tablespoons canola oil
- 1 cup red onions, chopped
- 1 parsnip, chopped
- 1 red bell pepper, seeded and chopped
- 1 carrot, chopped
- 3 garlic cloves, minced
- 1 pound dried red beans, soaked and rinsed
- 5 cups beef bone broth
- 1 teaspoon dried oregano
- 1 teaspoon dried sage
- 1 teaspoon dried rosemary
- Kosher salt and freshly ground black pepper, to taste
- 2 bay leaves

Directions

1. Press the "BROWN/SAUTÉ" button and set temperature to HIGH; press the "START/STOP" button. Now, heat the oil and sweat the onions until they are translucent.
2. Then, add the parsnip, bell pepper, carrot, and garlic; cook an additional 3 minutes or until the vegetables are softened.
3. Stir in the remaining ingredients.
4. Secure the lid and press the "SOUP" button. Press the "START/STOP" button; cook for 25 minutes at High pressure.
5. Once cooking is complete, use a natural pressure release and carefully remove the lid.
6. Discard bay leaves. You can purée the soup in your blender if desired. Let cool completely.

Storing

- Spoon your soup into airtight containers; keep in your refrigerator for up to 4 days.
- For freezing, place your soup in heavy-duty freezer bags. When the bags are frozen through, stack them up like file folders to save space in the freezer.
- Freeze up to 4 months. Defrost in the microwave or refrigerator. Bon appétit!

34. Traditional Chili with Cheese

You can't go wrong with a classic chili because it cooks perfectly in the Crock-Pot Express. Serve over hot rice if desired.

Servings 8

Ready in about 35 minutes

NUTRITIONAL INFORMATION (Per Serving)

300 - Calories
19.1g - Fat
9.7g - Carbs
22g - Protein
2.9g - Sugars

Ingredients

- 1 tablespoon lard
- 1 cup onion, chopped
- 3 garlic cloves, smashed
- 1/2 pound ground pork
- 1/2 pound ground beef
- 2 pounds red kidney beans, soaked overnight
- 2 cups tomato, puréed
- 1 cup onion, chopped
- 3 garlic cloves, smashed
- 2 bell peppers, deveined and chopped
- 1 cup water
- 1 cup chicken stock
- Sea salt and freshly ground black pepper, to taste
- 1 teaspoon cayenne pepper
- 1 teaspoon red chili powder
- 1 teaspoon Mexican oregano
- 1 bay leaf
- 1 cup Pepper-Jack cheese, grated

Directions

1. Press the "BROWN/SAUTÉ" button and set temperature to HIGH; press the "START/STOP" button. Now, melt the lard and cook the onion until tender and translucent.
2. Add the garlic and ground meat; continue to cook until the meat is delicately browned.
3. Now, stir in the beans, tomato, onion, garlic, peppers, water, stock, salt, black pepper, cayenne pepper, chili powder, oregano and bay leaf.
4. Secure the lid and press the "SOUP" button. Press the "BEANS/CHILI" button; cook for 30 minutes at High pressure.
5. Once cooking is complete, use a natural pressure release and carefully remove the lid. Top with grated cheese. Let cool completely.

Storing

- Spoon your chili into airtight containers or Ziploc bags; keep in your refrigerator for up to 3 to 4 days.
- For freezing, place your chili in airtight containers. It will maintain the best quality for about 4 to 6 months. Defrost in the refrigerator. Bon appétit!

35. Country Pork Soup with Spinach

Pork soup with vegetable is the ultimate comfort food. You can make a double batch and easily freeze the leftovers for later.

Servings 4

Ready in about 40 minutes

NUTRITIONAL INFORMATION (Per Serving)

264 - Calories
8.6g - Fat
6.6g - Carbs
38.2g - Protein
2.5g - Sugars

Ingredients

- 1 tablespoon olive oil
- 1 pound pork stew meat, cubed
- 4 cups beef bone broth
- 1 cup scallion, chopped
- 1 carrot, sliced
- 1 celery, sliced
- 1 turnip, peeled and sliced
- Sea salt and ground black pepper, to taste
- 2 cups spinach

Directions

1. Press the "BROWN/SAUTÉ" button and set temperature to HIGH; press the "START/STOP" button. Heat the oil and sear the meat until it is delicately browned.
2. Add the remaining ingredients, except for spinach.
3. Secure the lid and press the "SOUP" button. Press the "START/STOP" button; cook for 30 minutes at High pressure.
4. Once cooking is complete, use a quick pressure release and carefully remove the lid.
5. Add spinach to the Crock-Pot Express; seal the lid and allow it to sit in the residual heat until wilted. Let cool completely.

Storing

- Spoon your soup into airtight containers; keep in your refrigerator for up to 4 days.
- For freezing, place your soup in heavy-duty freezer bags. When the bags are frozen through, stack them up like file folders to save space in the freezer.
- Freeze up to 4 months. Defrost in the microwave or refrigerator. Bon appétit!

36. Easy Pork Carnitas

With Crock-Pot Express pork, your family lunch becomes a breeze! Serve on hamburger buns with coleslaw on the side.

Servings 8

Ready in about 35 minutes

NUTRITIONAL INFORMATION (Per Serving)

434 - Calories
25.2g - Fat
13.6g - Carbs
36.1g - Protein
10.5g - Sugars

Ingredients

- 2 ½ pounds pork butt, cut into bite-sized cubes
- 1/2 cup vegetable broth
- 1/2 cup barbecue sauce
- Sea salt and ground black pepper
- 1 teaspoon dried oregano
- 1/2 teaspoon dried basil
- 1 tablespoon maple syrup
- 1 red chili pepper, minced
- 1 cooking apple, cored and diced

Directions

1. Add pork, broth, barbecue sauce, salt, black pepper, oregano, basil, maple syrup, chili pepper, and apple to your Crock-Pot Express.
2. Secure the lid and press the "SOUP" button. Press the "START/STOP" button; cook for 30 minutes at High pressure.
3. Once cooking is complete, use a natural pressure release and carefully remove the lid.
4. Shred the pork with two forks. Return it back to the Crock-Pot Express. Let cool completely.

Storing

- Place the pork in an airtight container; keep in your refrigerator for 3 to 5 days.
- For freezing, place the pork in airtight containers or heavy-duty freezer bags. Freeze up to 4 to 6 months. Defrost in the refrigerator. Reheat in your oven at 250 degrees F until heated through. Bon appétit!

37. Pork Chop Soup

Here is a complete meal in a bowl. This hearty soup is loaded with market-fresh vegetables and succulent pork chops for a well-balanced meal.

Servings 4

Ready in about 40 minutes

NUTRITIONAL INFORMATION (Per Serving)

444 - Calories
16.9g - Fat
42.2g - Carbs
31.6g - Protein
5.1g - Sugars

Ingredients

- 2 tablespoons vegetable oil
- 3/4 pound bone-in pork chops
- 1/2 cup sweet onion, chopped
- 1 teaspoon fresh garlic, crushed
- 2 sweet peppers, deveined and chopped
- 4 potatoes, peeled and diced
- 2 carrots, trimmed and thinly sliced
- 1 parsnip, trimmed and thinly sliced
- 4 cups vegetable broth, preferably homemade
- Salt and freshly ground black pepper, to taste
- 1/2 teaspoon paprika
- 1 teaspoon dried thyme
- 1 (1/2-inch) piece fresh ginger, grated
- 1 (1.41-ounce) package tamarind soup base

Directions

1. Press the "BROWN/SAUTÉ" button and set temperature to HIGH; press the "START/STOP" button. Then, heat the vegetable oil and brown pork chops for 4 minutes on each side.
2. Secure the lid and press the "SOUP" button. Press the "START/STOP" button; cook for 30 minutes at High pressure.
3. Once cooking is complete, use a natural pressure release and carefully remove the lid. Let cool completely.

Storing

- Spoon your soup into airtight containers; keep in your refrigerator for up to 4 days.
- For freezing, place your soup in heavy-duty freezer bags. When the bags are frozen through, stack them up like file folders to save space in the freezer.
- Freeze up to 4 months. Defrost in the microwave or refrigerator. Bon appétit!

38. Pilaf with Tomato and Carp

The easiest way to make lunch is with one-pot meals. A teaspoon of capers will elevate this pilaf from simple to extraordinary.

Servings 4

Ready in about 15 minutes

NUTRITIONAL INFORMATION (Per Serving)

336 - Calories
16.7g - Fat
28.4g - Carbs
28.6g - Protein
8.8g - Sugars

Ingredients

- 1 tablespoon olive oil
- 1 cup chicken stock
- 1 cup tomato paste
- 1 teaspoon dried rosemary, crushed
- 1 tablespoon dried parsley
- 1/2 teaspoon dried marjoram leaves
- Sea salt and ground black pepper, to taste
- 1/2 teaspoon dried oregano leaves
- 1 cup Arborio rice
- 1 pound carp, chopped

Directions

1. Simply throw all of the above ingredients into your Crock-Pot Express.
2. Secure the lid and press the "RICE/RISOTTO" button. Press the "START/STOP" button; cook for 6 minutes at High pressure.
3. Once cooking is complete, use a quick pressure release and carefully remove the lid.
4. Let cool completely.

Storing

- Spoon your pilaf into airtight containers or Ziploc bags; keep in your refrigerator for up to 4 to 6 days.
- For freezing, place your pilaf in airtight containers. Freeze up to 6 months. Defrost in the refrigerator. Bon appétit!

39. Tuna Chowder with Green Pea

Crispy, fried ham, tuna steaks, and green peas combine to create the perfect seafood chowder that your family will love! Double cream is the perfect thing to thicken the chowder and makes it richer.

Servings 5

Ready in about 15 minutes

NUTRITIONAL INFORMATION (Per Serving)

360 - Calories
11.2g - Fat
25.7g - Carbs
38.5g - Protein
9.6g - Sugars

Ingredients

- 2 tablespoons olive oil
- 4 slices ham, chopped
- 1 cup shallots, chopped
- 2 cloves garlic, minced
- 2 carrots, chopped
- 5 cups seafood stock
- 1 ¼ pounds tuna steak, diced
- Sea salt and ground black pepper, to taste
- 1 teaspoon cayenne pepper
- 1/2 teaspoon ground bay leaf
- 1/2 teaspoon mustard powder
- 1 ½ cups double cream
- 1 ½ cups frozen green peas

Directions

1. Press the "BROWN/SAUTÉ" button and set temperature to HIGH; press the "START/STOP" button. Heat the oil and fry the ham until crispy.
2. Then, add the shallot and garlic; continue to cook an additional 2 minutes or until tender and fragrant.
3. Add the carrot, stock, tuna, salt, black pepper, cayenne pepper, ground bay leaf, and mustard powder.
4. Secure the lid and press the "SOUP" button. Press the "START/STOP" button; cook for 6 minutes at High pressure.
5. Once cooking is complete, use a natural pressure release and carefully remove the lid.
6. Add double cream and frozen peas. Press the "BROWN/SAUTÉ" button again and cook for a couple of minutes more or until heated through. Let cool completely.

Storing

- Spoon your chowder into airtight containers; keep in your refrigerator for up to 4 days.
- For freezing, place your chowder in heavy-duty freezer bags. When the bags are frozen through, stack them up like file folders to save space in the freezer.
- Freeze up to 4 to 6 months. Defrost in the microwave or refrigerator. Bon appétit!

40. Japanese-Style Rice Stew

If you like Japanese flavors, you will love this Western-style Japanese beef and rice. You can use Asian mushrooms and Japanese rice for an authentic experience.

Servings 6

Ready in about 30 minutes

NUTRITIONAL INFORMATION (Per Serving)

368 - Calories
16.1g - Fat
30.9g - Carbs
25.5g - Protein
3g - Sugars

Ingredients

- 1 tablespoon lard, at room temperature
- 1 ½ pounds ribeye steaks, cut into bite-sized pieces
- 1/2 cup shallots, chopped
- 4 cloves garlic, minced
- Salt and black pepper, to taste
- 1/2 teaspoon sweet paprika
- 1 sprig dried thyme, crushed
- 1 sprig dried rosemary, crushed
- 1 carrot, chopped
- 1 celery stalk, chopped
- 1/4 cup tomato paste
- 2 cups beef bone broth
- 1/3 cup rice wine
- 1 tablespoon Tonkatsu sauce
- 1 cup brown rice

Directions

1. Press the "BROWN/SAUTÉ" button and set temperature to HIGH; press the "START/STOP" button.
2. Now, heat the oil and cook the beef until it is delicately browned. Add the remaining ingredients; stir to combine.
3. Secure the lid and press the "RICE/RISOTTO" button. Press the "START/STOP" button; cook for 25 minutes at High pressure.
4. Once cooking is complete, use a natural pressure release and carefully remove the lid.
5. Let cool completely.

Storing

- Spoon rice stew into airtight containers or Ziploc bags; keep in your refrigerator for up to 4 to 6 days.
- For freezing, place rice stew in airtight containers. Freeze up to 6 months. Defrost in the refrigerator. Bon appétit!

DINNER

41. Duck Breast with Mushrooms

Cook this satisfying poultry recipe with all of your favorites: duck breasts, Port wine, and wild mushrooms. Amazing!

Servings 4

Ready in about 30 minutes

NUTRITIONAL INFORMATION (Per Serving)

203 - Calories
8.5g - Fat
5.5g - Carbs
26.5g - Protein
2.7g - Sugars

Ingredients

- 1 pound duck breast, sliced
- 1/2 teaspoon red chili pepper
- 1 teaspoon cayenne pepper
- 1/2 teaspoon sea salt
- 1/2 teaspoon mustard powder
- 1/2 teaspoon freshly ground black pepper
- 1 tablespoon tallow, melted
- 1/4 cup Port wine
- 2 medium-sized shallots, sliced
- 2 garlic cloves, minced
- 1 (1-inch) piece fresh ginger, peeled and grated
- 1 pound wild mushrooms, sliced
- 1 cup water
- 1 mushroom soup cube

Directions

1. Season duck breast with chili pepper, cayenne pepper, salt, mustard powder, and black pepper.
2. Press the "BROWN/SAUTÉ" button and set temperature to HIGH; press the "START/STOP" button. Then, melt the tallow. Sear the seasoned duck for 4 to 6 minutes, turning periodically; set it aside.
3. Pour in Port wine to scrape up any brown bits from the bottom of the Crock-Pot Express. Stir in the remaining ingredients.
4. Secure the lid and press the "POULTRY" button. Press the "START/STOP" button; cook for 15 minutes at High pressure.
5. Once cooking is complete, use a quick pressure release and carefully remove the lid. Let cool completely.

Storing

- Place the duck and mushrooms in airtight containers or Ziploc bags; keep in your refrigerator for 3 to 4 days.
- For freezing, place the duck and mushrooms in airtight containers or heavy-duty freezer bags. It will maintain the best quality for about 2 to 3 months. Defrost in the refrigerator. Enjoy!

42. Chicken with Two-Cheese Sauce

Prepare this chicken recipe and start your week off right! Seriously, chicken breast with cheese sauce will blow your mind.

Servings 4

Ready in about 20 minutes

NUTRITIONAL INFORMATION (Per Serving)

268 - Calories
14.9g - Fat
1.5g - Carbs
30.5g - Protein
0.8g - Sugars

Ingredients

- 1 tablespoon olive oil
- 4 chicken breasts halves
- 1/4 teaspoon ground black pepper, or more to taste
- 1/4 teaspoon ground bay leaf
- 1/2 teaspoon dried basil
- Salt, to taste
- 1 teaspoon dried marjoram
- 1 cup water

Cheese Sauce:
- 2 tablespoons mayonnaise
- 1/2 cup Gruyère cheese, grated
- 1/2 cup Cottage cheese, at room temperature
- 1 teaspoon garlic powder
- 1/2 teaspoon porcini powder

Directions

1. Press the "BROWN/SAUTÉ" button and set temperature to HIGH; press the "START/STOP" button; heat the oil. Once hot, sear the chicken breasts for 2 minutes per side.
2. Add black pepper, ground bay leaf, dried basil, salt, and marjoram; pour in the water.
3. Secure the lid and press the "POULTRY" button. Press the "START/STOP" button; cook for 15 minutes at High pressure.
4. Once cooking is complete, use a natural pressure release and carefully remove the lid.
5. Clean the Crock-Pot Express. Press the "BROWN/SAUTÉ" button and set temperature to HIGH; press the "START/STOP" button. Add the sauce ingredients and stir until everything is heated through.
6. Top the chicken with the sauce. Let cool completely.

Storing

- Place chicken and sauce in airtight containers or Ziploc bags; keep in your refrigerator for 3 to 4 days.
- For freezing, place chicken and sauce in airtight containers or heavy-duty freezer bags. It will maintain the best quality for about 4 months. Defrost in the refrigerator. Enjoy!

43. Brussels Sprouts with Romano Cheese

Accompany your dinner with cheesy Brussels sprouts! You can also serve this fabulous dish as a complete vegetarian meal.

Servings 4

Ready in about 20 minutes

NUTRITIONAL INFORMATION (Per Serving)

261 - Calories
16.2g - Fat
20.1g - Carbs
13.2g - Protein
4.1g - Sugars

Ingredients

- 1 ½ pounds Brussels sprouts, trimmed
- 3 tablespoons ghee
- 2 garlic cloves, minced
- 1/2 cup scallions, finely chopped
- Salt, to taste
- 1/2 teaspoon freshly ground black pepper
- 1/2 teaspoon red pepper flakes
- 1 cup Romano cheese, grated

Directions

1. Place 1 cup of water and a steamer basket on the bottom of your Crock-Pot Express. Place Brussels sprouts in the steamer basket.
2. Secure the lid and press the "STEAM" button. Press the "START/STOP" button; cook for 5 minutes at High pressure.
3. Once cooking is complete, use a quick pressure release and carefully remove the lid.
4. While Brussels sprouts are still hot, add ghee, garlic, scallions, salt, black pepper, red pepper, and Romano cheese; toss to coat well. Let cool completely.

Storing

- Place Brussels sprout in airtight containers or Ziploc bags; keep in your refrigerator for 3 to 5 days.
- Place Brussels sprout in freezable containers; they can be frozen for up to 3 months. Defrost in the refrigerator or microwave. Enjoy!

44. Chicken with Cheese-Parsley Dip

This parsley dipping sauce makes chicken drumsticks exciting again. And remember – anything pork can do, chicken can do better!

Servings 6

Ready in about 1 hour 20 minutes

NUTRITIONAL INFORMATION (Per Serving)

468 - Calories
37.8g - Fat
2.1g - Carbs
28.7g - Protein
0.7g - Sugars

Ingredients

- 2 garlic cloves, minced
- 1 cup dry white wine
- 1 red chili pepper
- Sea salt and ground black pepper, to taste
- 1/4 cup sesame oil
- 6 chicken drumsticks

Parsley Dip:
- 1/2 cup fresh parsley leaves, chopped
- 1/3 cup cream cheese
- 1/3 cup mayonnaise
- 1 garlic clove, minced
- 1/2 teaspoon cayenne pepper
- 1 tablespoon fresh lime juice

Directions

1. Place garlic, whine, chili pepper, salt, black pepper, and sesame oil in a ceramic container. Add chicken drumsticks; let them marinate for 1 hour in your refrigerator.
2. Add the chicken drumsticks, along with the marinade, to the Crock-Pot Express.
3. Secure the lid and press the "POULTRY" button. Press the "START/STOP" button; cook for 15 minutes at High pressure.
4. Once cooking is complete, use a quick pressure release and carefully remove the lid.
5. In a mixing bowl, thoroughly combine parsley, cream cheese mayonnaise, garlic, cayenne pepper, and lime juice. Let cool completely.

Storing

- Place the chicken in airtight containers or Ziploc bags; keep in your refrigerator for up to 3 to 4 days.
- For freezing, place the chicken in airtight containers or heavy-duty freezer bags. Freeze up to 4 months.
- Once thawed in the refrigerator, heat in the preheated oven at 375 degrees F for 20 to 25 minutes or until heated through.
- Refrigerate the sauce in covered container for 3 to 4 days. Enjoy!

45. Fish and Veggie Skewers

Check to ensure ingredients are desired doneness; if not
seal the lid again and cook a few minutes more.

Servings 4

**Ready in about
15 minutes**

**NUTRITIONAL
INFORMATION
(Per Serving)**

263 - Calories
15.1g - Fat
6.4g - Carbs
24.8g - Protein
3.7g - Sugars

Ingredients

- 1/2 pound yellow squash zucchini, cubed
- 1 red onion, cut into wedges
- 2 bell peppers, cut into strips
- 1 pound salmon, skinned, deboned and cut into bite-sized chunks
- 2 tablespoons toasted sesame oil
- Sea salt and ground black pepper, to taste
- 1 teaspoon red pepper flakes
- 8 sticks fresh rosemary, lower leaves removed

Directions

1. Prepare your Crock-Pot Express by adding 1½ cups of water and metal rack to its bottom.
2. Thread vegetables and fish alternately onto rosemary sticks.
3. Drizzle with sesame oil; sprinkle with salt, black pepper, and red pepper flakes. Cover with a piece of foil.
4. Secure the lid and press the "RICE/RISOTTO" button. Press the "START/STOP" button; cook for 6 minutes at High pressure.
5. Once cooking is complete, use a quick pressure release and carefully remove the lid. Let cool completely.

Storing

- Place fish and vegetables in airtight containers; they will last for 3 to 4 days in the refrigerator.
- For freezing, place fish and vegetables in airtight containers or heavy-duty freezer bags. Freeze up to 2 to 3 months. Defrost in the microwave or refrigerator. Bon appétit!

46. Saucy Pork Picnic Shoulder

A minimum internal temperature of picnic shoulder should be 175 degrees F. For the complete experience, serve with roasted new potatoes.

Servings 4

Ready in about 55 minutes

NUTRITIONAL INFORMATION (Per Serving)

288 - Calories
12.7g - Fat
6.1g - Carbs
35.2g - Protein
3.2g - Sugars`

Ingredients

- 1 ½ pounds pork picnic shoulder
- 1 teaspoon garlic powder
- 1/2 teaspoon cumin powder
- 1/4 teaspoon cinnamon, ground
- 1 teaspoon celery seeds
- 1 teaspoon oregano, dried
- Sea salt and ground black pepper, to taste
- 1/2 cup fresh orange juice
- 1 cup beef bone broth

Directions

1. Place all of the above ingredients in the Crock-Pot Express.
2. Secure the lid and press the "MEAT/STEW" button; press the "START/STOP" button; cook for 50 minutes at High pressure.
3. Once cooking is complete, use a natural pressure release and carefully remove the lid.
4. Test for doneness and thinly slice the pork. Let cool completely.

Storing

- Place the pork in airtight containers or Ziploc bags; keep in your refrigerator for up to 3 to 4 days.
- For freezing, place the pork in airtight containers or heavy-duty freezer bags. Freeze up to 2 to 3 months. Defrost in the refrigerator. Bon appétit!

47. Mexican-Style Pork

This Mexican-inspired dish provides a unique menu opportunity for you and your family! Really tasty!

Servings 8

Ready in about 45 minutes

NUTRITIONAL INFORMATION (Per Serving)

503 - Calories
30.4g - Fat
11.6g - Carbs
42.6g - Protein
2.9g - Sugars

Ingredients

- 1 heaping tablespoon lard, melted
- 1 cup shallots, chopped
- 2 cloves garlic, sliced
- 2 pounds pork butt, cut into 2-inch pieces
- 2 sprigs thyme, leaves chopped
- 1/2 teaspoon cumin
- 1 teaspoon Mexican oregano
- Sea salt and ground black pepper, to taste
- 4 cups chicken bone broth
- 1/2 cup fresh ripe tomato, puréed
- 2 bay leaves
- 1 celery with leaves, chopped
- 2 dried ancho chiles, chopped
- 1 red bell pepper, thinly sliced
- 1 (15-ounce) can white hominy, drained and rinsed

Directions

1. Press the "BROWN/SAUTÉ" button and set temperature to HIGH; press the "START/STOP" button. Now, melt the lard. Once hot, sauté the shallots and garlic until they are tender and fragrant.
2. Add the pork and cook an additional 3 minutes or until it is delicately browned. Add the remaining ingredients and gently stir to combine.
3. Secure the lid and press the "MEAT/STEW" button; press the "START/STOP" button; cook for 40 minutes at High pressure.
4. Once cooking is complete, use a natural pressure release and carefully remove the lid. Let cool completely.

Storing

- Place the pork in airtight containers or Ziploc bags; keep in your refrigerator for up to 3 to 4 days.
- For freezing, place the pork in airtight containers or heavy-duty freezer bags. Freeze up to 2 to 3 months. Defrost in the refrigerator. Bon appétit!

48. Cheese-Stuffed Meatballs

Kids of all ages will love these meatballs! Don't forget to add your favorite chili powder for some extra oomph.

Servings 6

Ready in about 15 minutes

NUTRITIONAL INFORMATION (Per Serving)

404 - Calories
24.9g - Fat
9.6g - Carbs
35.3g - Protein
3.1g - Sugars

Ingredients

- 1 ½ pounds ground turkey
- 2 eggs
- 1 yellow onion, chopped
- 2 garlic cloves, minced
- 1 cup tortilla chips, crumbled
- 1/2 teaspoon paprika
- Kosher salt, to taste
- 1/4 teaspoon freshly ground black pepper
- 1/2 teaspoon dried basil
- 1/2 teaspoon dried oregano
- 8 ounces Swiss cheese, cubed
- 1 tablespoon olive oil
- 1/2 cup tomato, pureed
- 1/2 cup water
- 1 tablespoon sugar
- 1/2 teaspoon chili powder

Directions

1. Thoroughly combine ground turkey, eggs, onion, garlic, crumbled tortilla chips, paprika, salt, pepper, basil, and oregano.
2. Roll the mixture into meatballs. Press 1 cheese cube into center of each meatball, sealing it inside.
3. Press the "BROWN/SAUTÉ" button and set temperature to HIGH; press the "START/STOP" button; now, heat the olive oil.
4. Brown the meatballs for a couple of minutes, turning them periodically. Add the tomato sauce, water, sugar, and chili powder.
5. Secure the lid and press the "SOUP" button; press the "START/STOP" button; cook for 10 minutes at High pressure.
6. Once cooking is complete, use a quick pressure release and carefully remove the lid. Let cool completely.

Storing

- Place the meatballs in airtight containers or Ziploc bags; keep in your refrigerator for up to 3 to 4 days.
- Freeze the meatballs in airtight containers or heavy-duty freezer bags. Freeze up to 3 to 4 months. To defrost, slowly reheat in a saucepan. Bon appétit!

49. Chicken Casserole with Mayo and Cheese

This cheese and chicken casserole might earn a permanent spot in your weekly meal plan. Regular, full-fat mayonnaise is a perfect addition to this surprisingly delicious dish.

Servings 6

Ready in about 30 minutes

NUTRITIONAL INFORMATION (Per Serving)

424 - Calories
28.7g - Fat
7.2g - Carbs
33.2g - Protein
2.8g - Sugars

Ingredients

- 2 tablespoons butter
- 1 ½ pounds chicken breasts
- 2 garlic cloves, halved
- 1 teaspoon cayenne pepper
- 1/2 teaspoon mustard powder
- Sea salt, to taste
- 1/2 teaspoon ground black pepper
- 8 ounces Cheddar cheese, sliced
- 1/2 cup mayonnaise
- 1 cup Parmesan cheese, grated

Directions

1. Press the "BROWN/SAUTÉ" button and set temperature to HIGH; press the "START/STOP" button. Melt the butter; sear the chicken for 2 to 3 minutes per side.
2. Add garlic and continue to sauté for 30 seconds more. Season with cayenne pepper, mustard powder, salt, and black pepper.
3. Add cheddar cheese and mayonnaise; top with grated Parmesan cheese.
4. Secure the lid and press the "SOUP" button; cook for 20 minutes at High pressure. Once cooking is complete, use a quick pressure release and carefully remove the lid. Let cool completely.

Storing

- Slice the casserole into six pieces and place in airtight containers; it will last for 3 to 4 days in the refrigerator.
- For freezing, place each portion in a separate heavy-duty freezer bag. Freeze up to 4 to 6 months. Defrost in the microwave or refrigerator. Bon appétit!

50. Beef Brisket with Sweet Sauce

The beef brisket, as one of the beef primal cuts, cooks perfectly in the Crock-Pot Express. Sweet Riesling sauce makes a great addition to the braised beef brisket.

Servings 6

**Ready in about
1 hour
5 minutes**

**NUTRITIONAL
INFORMATION
(Per Serving)**

338 - Calories
21.7g - Fat
15.5g - Carbs
18.4g - Protein
10.4g - Sugars

Ingredients

- 2 tablespoons olive oil
- 1 ½ pounds beef brisket
- 3 cloves garlic, minced or pressed
- 1 tablespoon Worcestershire sauce
- 1 celery, diced
- 1 carrot, diced
- 1 onion, cut into wedges
- 1 cup vegetable broth
- 1 tablespoon honey
- 1/4 cup late-harvest Riesling
- 1/3 cup dried apricots, chopped

Directions

1. Press the "BROWN/SAUTÉ" button and set temperature to HIGH; press the "START/STOP" button. Heat the olive oil. Once hot, cook beef brisket until it is delicately browned on all sides.
2. Add the remaining ingredients, except for dried apricots, to the Crock-Pot Express.
3. Secure the lid and press the "MEAT/STEW" button; press the "START/STOP" button; cook for 60 minutes at High pressure.
4. Once cooking is complete, use a natural pressure release and carefully remove the lid. Garnish with dried apricots. Let cool completely.

Storing

- Place the beef along with the sauce in airtight containers; keep in your refrigerator for 3 to 4 days.
- For freezing, place the beef along with the sauce in airtight containers or heavy-duty freezer bags. Freeze up to 2 to 3 months. Defrost in the microwave. Bon appétit!

51. Spicy Shredded Beef

This recipe calls for salsa, preferably homemade. Other taco fixings include diced avocado, Guacamole, sour cream, pickled cabbage, Pico de Gallo and so forth.

Servings 8

Ready in about 50 minutes

NUTRITIONAL INFORMATION (Per Serving)

250 - Calories
11.6g - Fat
6.1g - Carbs
31.4g - Protein
3.1g - Sugars

Ingredients

- 1 tablespoon corn oil
- 2 pounds chuck roast, cut into pieces
- 1 red onion, chopped
- 2 garlic cloves, minced
- 1 teaspoon ancho chili powder
- Sea salt and ground black pepper, to taste
- 1 teaspoon Mexican oregano
- 1/2 teaspoon coriander seeds
- 1/2 teaspoon fennel seeds
- 1 teaspoon mustard powder
- 2 cups tomato purée
- 1 cup water
- 2 beef bouillon cubes
- 1 cup salsa, to serve

Directions

1. Press the "BROWN/SAUTÉ" button and set temperature to HIGH; press the "START/STOP" button. Then, heat the oil. Brown the chuck roast for 3 minutes.
2. Add onion and garlic and cook an additional 2 minutes, stirring continuously. Stir in the remaining ingredients, except for salsa.
3. Secure the lid and press the "MEAT/STEW" button; press the "START/STOP" button; cook for 40 minutes at High pressure.
4. Once cooking is complete, use a natural pressure release and carefully remove the lid.
5. Remove beef from the Crock-Pot Express and let it cool slightly. After that, shred the meat using two forks.
6. Meanwhile, press the "BROWN/SAUTÉ" button again and simmer the cooking liquid until the sauce has reduced and thickened. Adjust the seasonings and return the shredded meat back to the Crock-Pot Express.
7. Top with salsa. Let cool completely.

Storing

- Place the beef in airtight containers; keep in your refrigerator for 3 to 4 days.
- For freezing, place the beef in airtight containers or heavy-duty freezer bags. Freeze up to 2 to 3 months. Defrost in the microwave. Bon appétit!

52. Sunday Beef Roast

Add vegetables and Chianti to the Instant Pot Crock-Pot Express and you will turn an ordinary roast into something spectacular! This recipe calls for Chianti but you can use Merlot and Pinot Noir and even white wines such as Pinot Grigio and Sancerre.

Servings 6

Ready in about 55 minutes

NUTRITIONAL INFORMATION (Per Serving)

363 - Calories
17.6g - Fat
6.1g - Carbs
41.6g - Protein
1.8g - Sugars

Ingredients

- 2 tablespoons olive oil
- 2 pounds beef roast
- 1 cup vegetable broth
- 1/2 cup Chianti
- Sea salt and ground black pepper, to taste
- 1 teaspoon red pepper flakes, crushed
- 1 cup shallots, chopped
- 2 cloves garlic, pressed
- 2 bay leaves
- 2 carrots, sliced
- 1 parsnip, sliced

Directions

1. Add the olive oil, beef, broth, Chianti, salt, black pepper, red pepper, shallots, garlic, and bay leaves to the Crock-Pot Express.
2. Secure the lid and press the "MEAT/STEW" button; press the "START/STOP" button; cook for 45 minutes at High pressure.
3. Once cooking is complete, use a quick pressure release and carefully remove the lid.
4. Then, add the carrots and parsnip to the Crock-Pot Express.
5. Secure the lid and press the "SOUP" button; press the "START/STOP" button; cook for 5 minutes at High pressure.
6. Once cooking is complete, use a quick pressure release and carefully remove the lid.
7. You can thicken the cooking liquid if desired. Let cool completely.

Storing

- Place the beef in airtight containers; keep in your refrigerator for 3 to 4 days.
- For freezing, place the beef in airtight containers or heavy-duty freezer bags. Freeze up to 2 to 3 months. Defrost in the microwave. Bon appétit!

53. Sirloin Steak with Hoisin Sauce

Here's the recipe for busy days when you don't have time to cook, but you want something special for your family.

Servings 8

Ready in about 1 hour

NUTRITIONAL INFORMATION (Per Serving)

283 - Calories
14.9g - Fat
10.9g - Carbs
24.8g - Protein
4.6g - Sugars

Ingredients

- 1 tablespoon lard, at room temperature
- 2 pounds boneless sirloin steak, thinly sliced
- Sea salt and ground black pepper, to your liking
- 1 teaspoon chili powder
- 2 tablespoons fresh parsley, chopped
- 1/2 cup red onion, sliced
- 2 garlic cloves, minced
- 2 sweet peppers, deveined and sliced
- 1/2 cup beef bone broth
- 1/2 cup hoisin sauce

Directions

1. Press the "BROWN/SAUTÉ" button and set temperature to HIGH; press the "START/STOP" button; melt the lard. Once hot, brown the sirloin steak for 6 minutes, flipping halfway through cooking time.
2. Season with salt and pepper; add chili powder, parsley, onion, garlic, and peppers. Pour in beef bone broth and secure the lid.
3. Secure the lid and press the "MEAT/STEW" button; press the "START/STOP" button; cook for 50 minutes at High pressure.
4. Once cooking is complete, use a natural pressure release and carefully remove the lid.
5. Shred the beef and return it to the Crock-Pot Express; stir to combine. Afterwards, pour hoisin sauce over shredded beef and vegetables. Let cool completely.

Storing

- Place the beef in airtight containers; keep in your refrigerator for 3 to 4 days.
- For freezing, place the beef in airtight containers or heavy-duty freezer bags. Freeze up to 2 to 3 months. Defrost in the microwave. Bon appétit!

54. One Pot Fish Risotto

This risotto is perfect for a potluck since it is easily transported. Feel free to use another combo of seasonings.

Servings 4

Ready in about 15 minutes

NUTRITIONAL INFORMATION (Per Serving)

432 - Calories
22.2g - Fat
32.2g - Carbs
42g - Protein
1.1g - Sugars

Ingredients

- 2 tablespoons butter, melted
- 1/2 cup leeks, sliced
- 2 garlic cloves, minced
- 2 cups basmati rice
- 1 ½ pounds sea bass fillets, diced
- 2 cups vegetable broth
- 1 cup water
- Salt, to taste
- 1/2 teaspoon ground black pepper
- 1 teaspoon fresh ginger, grated

Directions

1. Press the "BROWN/SAUTÉ" button and set temperature to HIGH; press the "START/STOP" button. Then, melt the butter and sweat the leeks for 2 to 3 minutes.
2. Stir in the garlic; continue to sauté an additional 40 seconds. Add the remaining ingredients.
3. Secure the lid and press the "RICE/RISOTTO" button. Press the "START/STOP" button; cook for 6 minutes at Low pressure.
4. Once cooking is complete, use a quick pressure release and carefully remove the lid. Let cool completely.

Storing

- Spoon your risotto into airtight containers or Ziploc bags; keep in your refrigerator for up to 4 to 6 days.
- For freezing, place your risotto in airtight containers. Freeze up to 6 months. Defrost in the refrigerator. Bon appétit!

55. Easy Trout Fillets

Ocean Trout is a powerhouse of heart-healthy omega-3 fatty acids. These home-style fish fillets will win your heart!

Servings 4

Ready in about 15 minutes

NUTRITIONAL INFORMATION (Per Serving)

122 - Calories
2.2g - Fat
1.6g - Carbs
22.7g - Protein
0.5g - Sugars

Ingredients

- 1 pound ocean trout fillets
- Sea salt, to taste
- 1 teaspoon caraway seeds
- 1/2 teaspoon mustard seeds
- 1/2 teaspoon paprika
- 1/2 cup spring onions, chopped
- 2 garlic cloves, minced
- 1 teaspoon mixed peppercorns
- 2 tablespoons champagne vinegar
- 1 tablespoon fish sauce
- 2 ½ cups broth, preferably homemade

Directions

1. Place the steaming basket and 1 ½ cups of water in your Crock-Pot Express. Sprinkle the ocean trout fillets with salt, caraway seeds, mustard seeds, and paprika.
2. Place the ocean trout fillet in the steaming basket. Add the other ingredients.
3. Secure the lid and press the "STEAM" button. Press the "START/STOP" button; cook for 3 minutes at Low pressure.
4. Once cooking is complete, a quick pressure release and carefully remove the lid. You can thicken the sauce if desired. Let cool completely.

Storing

- Place fish fillets in airtight containers; keep in your refrigerator for 3 to 4 days.
- For freezing, place fish fillets in airtight containers or heavy-duty freezer bags. Freeze up to 2 to 3 months. Defrost in the microwave. Bon appétit!

56. Mahi Mahi with Parmesan

This is the absolute best way to eat mahi-mahi fish. Mahi-mahi fish is loaded with antioxidants, protein, and selenium.

Servings 4

Ready in about 15 minutes

NUTRITIONAL INFORMATION (Per Serving)

376 - Calories
22.1g - Fat
9.4g - Carbs
34.2g - Protein
0.8g - Sugars

Ingredients

- 2 ripe tomatoes, sliced
- 1 teaspoon dried rosemary
- 1 teaspoon dried marjoram
- 1/2 teaspoon dried thyme
- 4 mahi-mahi fillets
- 2 tablespoons butter, at room temperature
- Sea salt and ground black pepper, to taste
- 8 ounces Parmesan cheese, freshly grated

Directions

1. Add 1 ½ cups of water and a rack to your Crock-Pot Express.
2. Spritz a casserole dish with a nonstick cooking spray. Arrange the slices of tomatoes on the bottom of the dish. Add the herbs.
3. Place mahi-mahi fillets on the top; drizzle the melted butter over the fish. Season it with salt and black pepper. Place the baking dish on the rack.
4. Secure the lid and press the "STEAM" button. Press the "START/STOP" button; cook for 9 minutes at Low pressure.
5. Once cooking is complete, a quick pressure release and carefully remove the lid. Top with parmesan and seal the lid again; allow the cheese to melt completely. Let cool completely.

Storing

- Place your fish in airtight containers; keep in your refrigerator for 3 to 4 days.
- For freezing, place your fish in airtight containers or heavy-duty freezer bags. Freeze up to 2 to 3 months. Defrost in the microwave. Bon appétit!

57. Mashed White Beans with Garlic

Adzuki beans are loaded with protein, antioxidants, iron, potassium and dietary fiber. They can protect your heart and prevent diabetes.

Servings 4

Ready in about 30 minutes

NUTRITIONAL INFORMATION (Per Serving)

95 - Calories
4.9g - Fat
7.7g - Carbs
6.4g - Protein
0.4g - Sugars

Ingredients

- 1 tablespoon canola oil
- 1/2 cup scallions, chopped
- 4 cloves garlic, smashed
- 1 ½ cups Adzuki beans
- 2 cups water
- 3 cups beef bone broth
- Sea salt and freshly ground black pepper, to taste
- 1 teaspoon paprika

Directions

1. Press the "BROWN/SAUTÉ" button and set temperature to HIGH; press the "START/STOP" button. Then, heat the oil and cook the scallions and garlic until tender; reserve.
2. Wipe down the Crock-Pot Express with a damp cloth. Add Adzuki beans, water, broth, salt, pepper, and paprika.
3. Secure the lid and press the "BEANS/CHILI" button. Press the "START/STOP" button; cook for 20 minutes at High pressure.
4. Once cooking is complete, use a natural pressure release and carefully remove the lid.
5. Transfer to your food processor and add the reserved scallion/garlic mixture. Then, process the mixture, working in batches. Process until smooth and uniform. Let cool completely.

Storing

- Spoon mashed beans into airtight containers or Ziploc bags; keep in your refrigerator for up to 3 to 4 days.
- For freezing, place mashed beans in airtight containers. It will maintain the best quality for about 4 to 6 months. Defrost in the refrigerator. Bon appétit!

58. Ground Beef Risotto

"Superfino" Carnaroli rice meets slightly browned ground beef in this Italian favorite. This risotto reheats well in the Crock-Pot Express.

Servings 4

Ready in about 15 minutes

NUTRITIONAL INFORMATION (Per Serving)

430 - Calories
26.3g - Fat
37.2g - Carbs
29.6g - Protein
4.2g - Sugars

Ingredients

- 2 tablespoons butter
- 1 cup shallots, diced
- 2 garlic cloves, minced
- 1/2 pound ground beef
- 2 bell peppers, seeded and chopped
- 1 red chili pepper, seeded and minced
- 2 cups Carnaroli rice, well-rinsed
- 4 cups beef stock
- A pinch of saffron
- Kosher salt and ground black pepper, to taste
- 1 teaspoon sweet paprika

Directions

1. Press the "BROWN/SAUTÉ" button and set temperature to HIGH; press the "START/STOP" button. Now, melt the butter; cook the shallots until they are softened.
2. Stir the garlic, ground beef, and peppers into your Crock-Pot Express. Continue to cook an additional 2 minutes or until the beef is no longer pink and peppers are tender.
3. Add rice, stock and seasonings to your Crock-Pot Express; gently stir to combine.
4. Secure the lid and press the "RICE/RISOTTO" button. Press the "START/STOP" button; cook for 6 minutes at High pressure.
5. Once cooking is complete, use a quick pressure release and carefully remove the lid. Let cool completely.

Storing

- Spoon beef risotto into airtight containers or Ziploc bags; keep in your refrigerator for up to 4 to 6 days.
- For freezing, place beef risotto in airtight containers. Freeze up to 6 months. Defrost in the refrigerator. Bon appétit!

59. Stuffed Peppers with Italian Sausage

These stuffed peppers will look so yummy on your dining table. Pick the peppers of different colors for even better presentation.

Servings 4

Ready in about 25 minutes

NUTRITIONAL INFORMATION (Per Serving)

478 - Calories
19.7g - Fat
65.6g - Carbs
19.6g - Protein
11.4g - Sugars

Ingredients

- 1 onion, chopped
- 2 cloves garlic, minced
- 1/2 pound Italian sausage, ground
- 1/2 pound button mushrooms, roughly chopped
- 3/4 cup buckwheat, soaked overnight
- 1 ½ cups chicken broth
- Salt and ground black pepper, to taste
- 1/2 teaspoon red pepper flakes, crushed
- 1 teaspoon dried basil
- 1/2 teaspoon dried oregano
- 4 medium-sized bell peppers, cored
- 2 (15-ounce) cans tomatoes
- 1/2 teaspoon mustard seeds

Directions

1. Press the "BROWN/SAUTÉ" button and set temperature to HIGH; press the "START/STOP" button. Once hot, add olive oil; now, sauté the onion and garlic until tender and aromatic.
2. Add Italian sausage and mushrooms; continue to cook an additional 2 minutes; reserve the sausage/mushroom mixture.
3. Now, add soaked buckwheat and chicken broth.
4. Secure the lid and press the "SOUP" button. Press the "START/STOP" button; cook for 5 minutes at High pressure.
5. Once cooking is complete, use a natural pressure release and carefully remove the lid.
6. Add the reserved sausage/mushroom mixture and seasonings; stir to combine well. Stuff the peppers. Wipe down the Crock-Pot Express with a damp cloth.
7. Add 1 ½ cups of water and metal rack to the Crock-Pot Express. Place stuffed peppers in a casserole dish; add tomatoes, mustard seeds, and bay leaf. Lower the dish onto the rack.
8. Secure the lid and press the "STEAM" button. Press the "START/STOP" button; cook for 10 minutes at High pressure.
9. Once cooking is complete, use a natural pressure release and carefully remove the lid. Let cool completely.

Storing

- Place stuffed peppers in airtight containers; keep in your refrigerator for 3 to 4 days.
- Wrap each stuffed pepper tightly in several layers of plastic wrap and squeeze the air out. Place them in airtight containers; they can be frozen for up to 1 month.
- To reheat, bake the thawed stuffed peppers at 200 degrees F until they are completely warm.

60. Spicy Yellow Lentils

—∿—

For a change of pace, serve lentils with pasta instead of rice. It is a good idea to serve with a dollop of a chilled sour cream.

Servings 5

Ready in about 20 minutes

NUTRITIONAL INFORMATION (Per Serving)

243 - Calories
4.8g - Fat
37.3g - Carbs
14.3g - Protein
2.3g - Sugars

Ingredients

- 1 tablespoon sesame oil
- 1/2 cup green onions, chopped
- 2 garlic cloves, minced
- 1 tablespoon fresh ginger, minced
- 1 bell pepper, chopped
- 1 habanero pepper, chopped
- 1 medium-sized carrot, chopped
- 1 1/3 cups yellow lentils, rinsed
- 1 teaspoon turmeric powder
- Salt and ground black pepper, to taste
- 1/2 teaspoon red pepper flakes
- 1/2 teaspoon fennel seeds
- 2 cups vegetable broth

Directions

1. Press the "BROWN/SAUTÉ" button and set temperature to HIGH; press the "START/STOP" button. Now, heat the oil and cook green onions, garlic, ginger, peppers, and carrot until they are softened.
2. Secure the lid and press the "BEANS/CHILI" button. Press the "START/STOP" button; cook for 15 minutes at High pressure.
3. Once cooking is complete, use a natural pressure release and carefully remove the lid. You can thicken the cooking liquid if desired. Let cool completely.

Storing

- Spoon yellow lentils into airtight containers or Ziploc bags; keep in your refrigerator for up to 5 to 7 days.
- For freezing, place yellow lentils in airtight containers. Freeze up to 6 months. Defrost in the refrigerator. Bon appétit!

VEGAN

61. Asian Brown Rice with Chickpeas

This ultra-simple Asian dish is healthy, nutritious and delicious. You should cook rice until it turns into a pudding-like consistency.

Servings 4

Ready in about 35 minutes

NUTRITIONAL INFORMATION (Per Serving)

366 - Calories
4.3g - Fat
70.5g - Carbs
11.7g - Protein
4.3g - Sugars

Ingredients

- 1 ½ cups brown rice
- 2 cups water
- 1 cup vegan dashi stock
- 1/2 teaspoon garlic powder
- Sea salt and ground black pepper, to taste
- 1/2 teaspoon cayenne pepper
- 1 (19-ounce) can chickpeas, drained
- 3 tablespoons shallots, chopped

Directions

1. Place brown rice, water, dashi stock, garlic powder, salt, black pepper, and cayenne pepper in the Crock-Pot Express; stir to combine well.
2. Secure the lid and press the "RICE/RISOTTO" button. Press the "START/STOP" button; cook for 30 minutes at High pressure.
3. Once cooking is complete, use a natural pressure release and carefully remove the lid.
4. Add canned chickpeas and stir to combine; seal the lid and let it sit until thoroughly warmed. Top with fresh shallots. Let cool completely.

Storing

- Spoon beef risotto into airtight containers or Ziploc bags; keep in your refrigerator for up to 4 to 6 days.
- For freezing, place beef risotto in airtight containers. Freeze up to 6 months. Defrost in the refrigerator. Bon appétit!

62. Vegan Mac and Cheese

A tasty side dish or complete lunch, it's up to you! Delight your vegan friends with this unique combination of pasta and creamy sauce.

Servings 4

Ready in about 15 minutes

NUTRITIONAL INFORMATION (Per Serving)

415 - Calories
11.5g - Fat
66g - Carbs
14.4g - Protein
6.7g - Sugars

Ingredients

- 1 (8-ounce) box elbow macaroni
- 3 Yukon gold potatoes, peeled and diced
- 1 yellow onion, chopped
- 1 garlic clove, minced
- 2 cups water
- 3 tablespoons nutritional yeast flakes
- Seasoned salt and ground black pepper, to taste
- 1/2 teaspoon red pepper flakes
- 1/2 cup cashews
- 1/3 cup almond milk

Directions

1. Place macaroni, potatoes, onion, garlic, and water in your Crock-Pot Express.
2. Secure the lid and press the "RICE/RISOTTO" button. Press the "START/STOP" button; cook for 6 minutes at High pressure.
3. Once cooking is complete, use a quick pressure release and carefully remove the lid.
4. Then, remove potatoes from cooking liquid using a slotted spoon; transfer them to your blender. Add nutritional yeast flakes, salt, black pepper, red pepper, cashews, and almond milk; blend until everything is creamy, uniform and smooth.
5. Add "cheese" mixture to the Crock-Pot Express; stir with warm pasta. Let cool completely.

Storing

- Spoon mac and cheese into airtight containers or Ziploc bags; keep in your refrigerator for up to 3 to 5 days.
- For freezing, place mac and cheese in airtight containers. Freeze up to 1 to 2 months. Defrost in the refrigerator. Bon appétit!

63. Autumn Soup with Corn and Noodles

A homey, veggie soup with flavorful, golden noodles.
A hearty, noodle soup always reminds us of grandma's
kitchen, right?

Servings 6

**Ready in about
20 minutes**

**NUTRITIONAL
INFORMATION
(Per Serving)**

194 - Calories
5.4g - Fat
29.9g - Carbs
8g - Protein
5.1g - Sugars

Ingredients

- 2 tablespoons olive oil
- 2 shallots, peeled and chopped
- 1 carrot, chopped
- 1 parsnip, chopped
- 1 turnip, chopped
- 3 garlic cloves, smashed
- 1 teaspoon cumin powder
- 1/2 teaspoon dried rosemary
- 1/2 teaspoon dried thyme
- 6 cups vegetable stock, preferably homemade
- 9 ounces vegan noodles
- 1 cup corn kernels
- Salt and freshly ground black pepper, to taste

Directions

1. Press the "BROWN/SAUTÉ" button and set temperature to HIGH; press the "START/STOP" button. Now, heat the oil and sauté the shallots with carrot, parsnip, and turnip until they have softened.
2. Stir in the garlic and cook an additional 40 seconds. Add cumin powder, rosemary, thyme, stock, and noodles.
3. Secure the lid and press the "SOUP" button. Press the "START/STOP" button; cook for 10 minutes at High pressure.
4. Once cooking is complete, use a quick pressure release and carefully remove the lid.
5. Add corn kernels, cover with the lid, and cook in the residual heat for 5 to 6 minutes more. Season with salt and pepper; taste and adjust the seasonings. Let cool completely.

Storing

- Spoon the soup into airtight containers; keep in your refrigerator for up to 4 days.
- For freezing, place the soup in airtight containers or heavy-duty freezer bags. Freeze up to 4 months.
- Defrost in the microwave or refrigerator. Bon appétit!

64. Vegetables with Peanut Sauce

Never underestimate the power of steamed vegetables. They are healthy, weight loss friendly, and extremely delicious.

Servings 4

Ready in about 15 minutes

NUTRITIONAL INFORMATION (Per Serving)

90 - Calories
4.3g - Fat
9.3g - Carbs
5.2g - Protein
4.3g - Sugars

Ingredients

- 1 ¼ cups water
- 1 pound broccoli florets
- 1 carrot, diced
- 1/2 teaspoon sea salt
- 1/2 teaspoon cayenne pepper
- 1/4 teaspoon ground white pepper

For the Sauce:
- 4 tablespoons silky peanut butter
- 3 tablespoons water
- 1 tablespoon champagne vinegar
- 1 tablespoons poppy seeds

Directions

1. Add 1 ¼ cups of water to the base of your Crock-Pot Express. Arrange broccoli and carrots in a steaming basket and transfer them to the Crock-Pot Express.
2. Secure the lid and press the "STEAM" button. Press the "START/STOP" button; cook for 3 minutes at High pressure.
3. Once cooking is complete, a quick pressure release and carefully remove the lid. Season your vegetables with salt, cayenne pepper, and ground white pepper.
4. Meanwhile, in a mixing bowl, thoroughly combine peanut butter, water, vinegar, and poppy seeds. Let cool completely.

Storing

- Divide the vegetables into four portions; divide the portions between four airtight containers; keep in your refrigerator for up 3 to 5 days.
- Place the sauce in the covered container; it will generally stay at the best quality for about 1 week.
- For freezing, wrap your vegetables tightly with plastic wrap and place in airtight containers. Freeze up to 10 to 12 months. Defrost in the refrigerator. Bon appétit!

65. The Best Vegan Chili Ever

This chili is quick, endlessly crave-worthy, and surprisingly delicious. A healthy, protein dish where vegetables and beans make a great blend.

Servings 6

Ready in about 15 minutes

NUTRITIONAL INFORMATION (Per Serving)

204 - Calories
6.5g - Fat
27.9g - Carbs
10.4g - Protein
6.9g - Sugars

Ingredients

- 2 tablespoons olive oil
- 1 red onion, chopped
- 3 cloves garlic minced or pressed
- 1 red bell pepper, diced
- 1 green bell pepper, diced
- 1 red chili pepper, minced
- Sea salt and ground black pepper, to taste
- 1 teaspoon cayenne pepper
- 1/2 teaspoon ground cumin
- 2 cups vegetable stock
- 2 ripe tomatoes, chopped
- 2 (15-ounce) cans beans, drained and rinsed
- 1 handful fresh cilantro leaves, chopped
- 1/2 cup tortilla chips

Directions

1. Press the "BROWN/SAUTÉ" button and set temperature to HIGH; press the "START/STOP" button. Now, heat the oil until sizzling.
2. Sauté the onion tender and translucent. Add garlic, peppers, salt, and pepper; continue to sauté until they are tender.
3. Now, stir in cayenne pepper, cumin, stock, tomatoes, and beans.
4. Secure the lid and press the "SOUP" button. Press the "START/STOP" button; cook for 10 minutes at High pressure.
5. Once cooking is complete, use a quick pressure release and carefully remove the lid. Top with fresh cilantro and tortilla chips. Let cool completely.

Storing

- Spoon your chili into airtight containers or Ziploc bags; keep in your refrigerator for up to 3 to 4 days.
- For freezing, place your chili in airtight containers. It will maintain the best quality for about 4 to 6 months. Defrost in the refrigerator. Bon appétit!

66. Restaurant-Style Hummus

Each ingredient in this dip plays a part in its rich and incredible flavor. Serve with pita bread and veggie sticks.

Servings 8

Ready in about 35 minutes

NUTRITIONAL INFORMATION (Per Serving)

186 - Calories
7.7g - Fat
22.8g - Carbs
7.6g - Protein
4g - Sugars

Ingredients

- 10 cups water
- 3/4 pound dried chickpeas, soaked
- 2 tablespoons tahini
- 1/2 lemon, juiced
- 1 teaspoon granulated garlic
- Salt and black pepper, to taste
- 1/3 teaspoon ground cumin
- 1/2 teaspoon cayenne pepper
- 1/2 teaspoon dried basil
- 3 tablespoon olive oil

Directions

1. Add water and chickpeas to the Crock-Pot Express. Secure the lid.
2. Secure the lid and press the "BEANS/CHILI" button. Press the "START/STOP" button; cook for 25 minutes at High pressure.
3. Once cooking is complete, use a natural pressure release and carefully remove the lid.
4. Now, drain your chickpeas, reserving the liquid. Transfer chickpeas to a food processor. Add tahini, lemon juice, and seasonings.
5. Puree until it is creamy; gradually pour in the reserved liquid and olive oil until the mixture is smooth and uniform. Let cool completely.

Storing

- Spoon your hummus into airtight containers; keep in your refrigerator for up to 4 to 7 days.
- For freezing, place your hummus in airtight containers or heavy-duty freezer bags. It will maintain the best quality for about 3 to 4 months. Defrost in the refrigerator. Bon appétit!

67. Green Bean and Mushroom Delight

This vegan dish is easy to prepare and it is packed with flavor and nutrition. Cooked with shiitake mushrooms and spices, this hearty meal can be served on any occasion.

Servings 4

Ready in about 25 minutes

NUTRITIONAL INFORMATION (Per Serving)

119 - Calories
7.6g - Fat
12.6g - Carbs
2.6g - Protein
2.6g - Sugars

Ingredients

- 2 cups water
- 6 dried shiitake mushrooms
- 2 tablespoons sesame oil
- 2 cloves garlic, minced
- 1/2 cup scallions, chopped
- 1 ½ pounds green beans, fresh or frozen (and thawed)
- 1/4 teaspoon ground black pepper
- 1/2 teaspoon red pepper flakes, crushed
- 1 bay leaf
- Sea salt, to taste

Directions

1. Press the "BROWN/SAUTÉ" button and set temperature to HIGH; press the "START/STOP" button. Bring the water to a rapid boil. Remove from the heat and add the dried shiitake mushrooms.
2. Allow the mushrooms to sit for 15 minutes to rehydrate. Then cut the mushrooms into slices; reserve the mushroom stock.
3. Wipe down the Crock-Pot Express with a kitchen cloth. Press the "BROWN/SAUTÉ" button to preheat your Crock-Pot Express. Once hot, heat the sesame oil.
4. Then, sauté the garlic and scallions until tender and aromatic. Add green beans, black pepper, red pepper, bay leaf, salt, reserved mushrooms and stock; stir to combine well.
5. Secure the lid and press the "STEAM" button. Press the "START/STOP" button; cook for 4 minutes at High pressure.
6. Once cooking is complete, a quick pressure release and carefully remove the lid.
7. Let cool completely.

Storing

- Divide green beans into four portions; divide the portions between four airtight containers; keep in your refrigerator for up 3 to 5 days.
- For freezing, place green beans in airtight containers. Freeze up to 10 to 12 months. Defrost in the refrigerator. Bon appétit!

68. Curried Rice with Tomatoes

Try one of the favorite risotto recipes that reheats well.
This risotto recipe is easy to follow and quick to prepare. It
might become a staple in your summer kitchen.

Servings 4

**Ready in about
25 minutes**

**NUTRITIONAL
INFORMATION
(Per Serving)**

251 - Calories
6.2g - Fat
44.1g - Carbs
4.2g - Protein
3g - Sugars

Ingredients

- 1 tablespoon sesame oil
- 1 yellow onion, peeled and chopped
- 2 cloves garlic, minced
- 1 cup tomatoes, pureed
- 1 carrot, chopped
- 1 tablespoon tomato powder
- 1 teaspoon curry powder
- 1 teaspoon citrus & ginger spice blend
- 1/2 teaspoon paprika
- Sea salt and freshly ground black pepper, to taste
- 1 cup white rice, soaked for 30 minutes
- 2 ½ cups water

Directions

1. Press the "BROWN/SAUTÉ" button and set temperature to HIGH; press the "START/STOP" button. Heat sesame oil until sizzling.
2. Sweat the onion for 2 to 3 minutes. Add garlic and cook an additional 30 to 40 seconds.
3. Add tomatoes and carrot; cook for a further 10 minutes, stirring periodically. Add seasonings, rice, and water to the Crock-Pot Express. Secure the lid.
4. Secure the lid and press the "RICE/RISOTTO" button. Press the "START/STOP" button; cook for 6 minutes at High pressure.
5. Once cooking is complete, use a natural pressure release and carefully remove the lid. Taste and adjust the seasonings.
6. Let cool completely.

Storing

- Spoon your rice into airtight containers or Ziploc bags; keep in your refrigerator for up to 4 to 6 days.
- For freezing, place your rice in airtight containers. Freeze up to 6 months. Defrost in the refrigerator. Bon appétit!

69. Red Lentils with Tomato

Lentils are protein packed food that can be used in various recipes. They cook fast in the Crock-Pot Express; they are easy to digest as well.

Servings 4

Ready in about 20 minutes

NUTRITIONAL INFORMATION (Per Serving)

405 - Calories
5.9g - Fat
67.5g - Carbs
24.5g - Protein
3.8g - Sugars

Ingredients

- 1 tablespoon olive oil
- 2 cups red lentils
- 1/2 cup scallions, finely chopped
- 1 teaspoon garlic, minced
- 1 teaspoon turmeric powder
- Sea salt and ground black pepper, to taste
- 1 teaspoon sweet paprika
- 1 (15-ounce) can tomatoes, crushed
- 1 bay leaf
- 1 handful fresh cilantro leaves, chopped

Directions

1. Add olive oil, lentils, scallions, garlic, turmeric, salt, black pepper, paprika, tomatoes, and bay leaf to your Crock-Pot Express.
2. Secure the lid and press the "SOUP" button. Press the "START/STOP" button; cook for 10 minutes at High pressure.
3. Once cooking is complete, use a natural pressure release and carefully remove the lid.
4. Discard bay leaf and spoon lentil into serving bowls. Top with fresh cilantro. Let cool completely.

Storing

- Spoon lentils into airtight containers or Ziploc bags; keep in your refrigerator for up to 5 to 7 days.
- For freezing, place lentils in airtight containers. Freeze up to 6 months. Defrost in the refrigerator. Bon appétit!

70. Mexican Sopa de Tomate

Pair cooked tomatoes with vegetables and pepitas and your taste buds will rejoice. This soup is perfect for a fancy Sunday lunch!

Servings 4

Ready in about 15 minutes

NUTRITIONAL INFORMATION (Per Serving)

125 - Calories
9.4g - Fat
8.1g - Carbs
4.2g - Protein
1.8g - Sugars

Ingredients

- 2 tablespoons olive oil
- 1/2 cup green onions, chopped
- 2 cloves garlic, crushed
- 2 carrots, roughly chopped
- 1 red chili pepper, seeded and chopped
- 1 pound ripe tomatoes, puréed
- 1 zucchini, chopped
- 1 teaspoon dried rosemary
- 1/2 teaspoon dried basil
- 1/2 teaspoon dried marjoram
- 1 teaspoon sweet paprika
- Sea salt and ground black pepper, to taste
- 1 cup vegetable stock
- 2 tablespoons fresh chives, chopped
- 2 tablespoons pepitas

Directions

1. Press the "BROWN/SAUTÉ" button and set temperature to HIGH; press the "START/STOP" button. Then, heat the oil until sizzling.
2. Now, cook green onions and garlic until tender and fragrant. Add carrots, chili pepper, tomatoes, zucchini, seasonings, and stock.
3. Secure the lid and press the "SOUP" button. Press the "START/STOP" button; cook for 6 minutes at High pressure.
4. Once cooking is complete, use a quick pressure release and carefully remove the lid. Then, purée the mixture with an immersion blender until the desired thickness is reached.
5. Add fresh chives and pepitas. Let cool completely.

Storing

- Spoon the soup into four airtight containers; keep in your refrigerator for up to 4 days.
- For freezing, place the soup in heavy-duty freezer bags. When the bags are frozen through, stack them up like file folders to save space in the freezer.
- Freeze up to 4 months. Defrost in the microwave or refrigerator. Bon appétit!

71. Chinese-Style Soup with Corn

Whether you're a vegan or not, you'll love this hearty vegetable soup. Serve with zha cai (pickled vegetables).

Servings 4

Ready in about 35 minutes

NUTRITIONAL INFORMATION (Per Serving)

177 - Calories
8.8g - Fat
18.5g - Carbs
7.8g - Protein
7.1g - Sugars

Ingredients

- 1 tablespoon toasted sesame oil
- 1 yellow onion, peeled and chopped
- 2 garlic cloves, minced
- 1 teaspoon fresh ginger, peeled and grated
- 1 jalapeño pepper, minced
- 1 celery stalk, chopped
- 2 carrots, chopped
- 1 teaspoon Five-spice powder
- Sea salt, to taste
- 1/2 teaspoon ground black pepper, to taste
- 1/2 teaspoon red pepper flakes
- 1 teaspoon dried parsley flakes
- 4 cups vegetable broth
- 2 ripe tomatoes, finely chopped
- 1 tablespoon soy sauce
- 1 cup sweet corn kernels, frozen and thawed
- 1 cup zha cai

Directions

1. Press the "BROWN/SAUTÉ" button and set temperature to HIGH; press the "START/STOP" button.
2. Once hot, add the oil. Sauté the onion, garlic, ginger and jalapeño pepper for 2 to 3 minutes, stirring occasionally.
3. Add the remaining ingredients, except for corn and zha cai; stir to combine well.
4. Secure the lid and press the "SOUP" button. Press the "START/STOP" button; cook for 25 minutes at High pressure.
5. Once cooking is complete, use a natural pressure release and carefully remove the lid.
6. After that, add corn and seal the lid again. Let it sit until heated through. Garnish with zha cai. Let cool completely.

Storing

- Spoon the soup into four airtight containers; keep in your refrigerator for up to 4 days.
- For freezing, place the soup in heavy-duty freezer bags. When the bags are frozen through, stack them up like file folders to save space in the freezer.
- Freeze up to 4 months. Defrost in the microwave or refrigerator. Bon appétit!

72. Curried Saucy Rice

Are you looking for a quick recipe to have on hand during your busy week? We've got a great recipe for you! You can double or triple the recipe, if desired.

Servings 3

Ready in about 20 minutes

NUTRITIONAL INFORMATION (Per Serving)

353 - Calories
9.6g - Fat
56.8g - Carbs
8g - Protein
1.7g - Sugars

Ingredients

- 1/4 cup water
- 2 cups vegetable broth
- 1 tablespoon olive oil
- 1 cup jasmine rice
- 1 tablespoon vegan margarine
- 1 yellow onion, chopped
- 1 teaspoon curry powder
- Fresh juice of 1/2 lemon
- Zest of 1/2 lemon
- Sea salt and ground black pepper, to taste

Directions

1. Place the water, 1 cup of vegetable broth, olive oil, and rice in your Crock-Pot Express.
2. Secure the lid and press the "RICE/RISOTTO" button. Press the "START/STOP" button; cook for 6 minutes at High pressure.
3. Once cooking is complete, use a natural pressure release and carefully remove the lid. Fluff the rice with a fork and reserve.
4. Wipe down the Crock-Pot Express with a kitchen cloth. Press the "BROWN/SAUTÉ" button and melt margarine. Then, sauté the onion until tender and translucent.
5. Add the remaining cup of vegetable broth, curry powder, lemon, salt, and black pepper. Press the "BROWN/SAUTÉ" button and stir until everything is incorporated.
6. Spoon the sauce over hot rice. Let cool completely.

Storing

- Spoon your rice into airtight containers or Ziploc bags; keep in your refrigerator for up to 4 to 6 days.
- For freezing, place your rice in airtight containers. Freeze up to 6 months. Defrost in the refrigerator. Bon appétit!

73. Spicy Thai Risotto

This recipe doesn't require some special ingredients. You can come up with a great meal using ingredients you already have in your kitchen.

Servings 3

Ready in about 20 minutes

NUTRITIONAL INFORMATION (Per Serving)

306 - Calories
16.7g - Fat
42.7g - Carbs
9.1g - Protein
18.2g - Sugars

Ingredients

- 1 cup basmati rice, rinsed
- 1 ¼ cups water
- Kosher salt and white pepper, to taste
- 2 tablespoons fresh coriander
- 4 ounces fresh green peas
- 2 fresh green chilies, chopped
- 1 garlic clove, pressed
- 1/2 cup candy onions, chopped
- 4 whole cloves
- 1/2 cup creamed coconut
- 1 tablespoon fresh lime juice

Directions

1. Combine all of the above ingredients, except for lime juice, in your Crock-Pot Express.
2. Secure the lid and press the "RICE/RISOTTO" button. Press the "START/STOP" button; cook for 6 minutes at High pressure.
3. Once cooking is complete, use a natural pressure release and carefully remove the lid. Drizzle with fresh lime juice. Let cool completely.

Storing

- Spoon your rice into airtight containers or Ziploc bags; keep in your refrigerator for up to 4 to 6 days.
- For freezing, place your rice in airtight containers. Freeze up to 6 months. Defrost in the refrigerator. Bon appétit!

74. Balkan-Style Refried Beans (Tavce Gravce)

Refried beans are always welcomed. You can buy cannellini beans in a can, but every now and then, it is a good idea to make an old-fashion version with dried and soaked beans.

Servings 6

Ready in about 35 minutes

NUTRITIONAL INFORMATION (Per Serving)

159 - Calories
10.1g - Fat
13.5g - Carbs
8.4g - Protein
3.2g - Sugars

Ingredients

- 2 tablespoons olive oil
- 1 yellow onion, chopped
- 2 garlic cloves, roughly chopped
- 2 medium-sized bell peppers, deveined and thinly sliced
- 1 teaspoon habanero pepper, minced
- 1 teaspoon dried rosemary
- 1/2 teaspoon ground cumin
- Salt and ground black pepper, to taste
- 1 ½ pounds dried Cannellini beans
- 2 bay leaves
- 6 cups water

Directions

1. Press the "BROWN/SAUTÉ" button and set temperature to HIGH; press the "START/STOP" button. Heat olive oil and cook the onion until tender and fragrant.
2. Now, add garlic and peppers; cook until they have softened, about 4 minutes. Add the remaining ingredients.
3. Secure the lid and press the "BEANS/CHILI" button. Press the "START/STOP" button; cook for 25 minutes at High pressure.
4. Once cooking is complete, use a natural pressure release and carefully remove the lid. Let cool completely.

Storing

- Spoon your chili into airtight containers or Ziploc bags; keep in your refrigerator for up to 3 to 4 days.
- For freezing, place your chili in airtight containers. It will maintain the best quality for about 4 to 6 months. Defrost in the refrigerator. Bon appétit!

75. Colorful Vegetable Congee

Get ready for a little piece of heaven. A gorgeous combo of fresh garden vegetables, wild rice, and spices.

Servings 4

Ready in about 35 minutes

NUTRITIONAL INFORMATION (Per Serving)

235 - Calories
8.1g - Fat
34.2g - Carbs
8.6g - Protein
6.3g - Sugars

Ingredients

- 2 tablespoons olive oil
- 1/2 cup leeks, roughly chopped
- 2 garlic cloves, minced
- 1 bell pepper, chopped
- 1 serrano pepper, chopped
- 2 carrots, chopped
- 1 fennel, diced
- 3/4 cup wild rice
- 1 cup tomato purée
- 2 cups water
- 2 cups vegetable broth
- 2 tablespoons fresh coriander, chopped
- 1 teaspoon fresh or dried rosemary
- Salt, to taste
- 1/2 teaspoon ground black pepper

Directions

1. Press the "BROWN/SAUTÉ" button and set temperature to HIGH; press the "START/STOP" button. Once hot, heat the oil.
2. Then, sauté the leeks, garlic, and pepper for 2 to 4 minutes, stirring periodically; add a splash of broth if needed.
3. Stir the remaining ingredients into your Crock-Pot Express; stir to combine well.
4. Secure the lid and press the "SOUP" button. Press the "START/STOP" button; cook for 30 minutes at High pressure.
5. Once cooking is complete, use a natural pressure release and carefully remove the lid.
6. Taste and adjust the seasonings. Let cool completely.

Storing

- Spoon the soup into four airtight containers; keep in your refrigerator for up to 4 days.
- For freezing, place the soup in heavy-duty freezer bags. When the bags are frozen through, stack them up like file folders to save space in the freezer.
- Freeze up to 4 months. Defrost in the microwave or refrigerator. Bon appétit!

76. Spicy Chowder with Cashew Cream

Make extremely creative and imaginative chowders in your Crock-Pot Express! This delicious chowder highlights the amazing taste of two types of peppers – bell pepper and serrano peppers.

Servings 4

Ready in about 15 minutes

NUTRITIONAL INFORMATION (Per Serving)

282 - Calories
22.2g - Fat
18.4g - Carbs
6.1g - Protein
7.9g - Sugars

Ingredients

- 3 teaspoons sesame oil
- 1/2 cup leeks, chopped
- 1 garlic clove, minced
- 1 celery with leaves, chopped
- 1 carrot, trimmed and chopped
- 1 red bell pepper, thinly sliced
- 1 green bell pepper, thinly sliced
- 1 serrano pepper, deveined and thinly sliced
- 4 ½ cups water
- Salt and ground black pepper, to taste
- 1 tablespoon soy sauce
- 1/2 cup raw cashews, soaked for 3 hours
- 1/2 cup almond milk, unsweetened

Directions

1. Press the "BROWN/SAUTÉ" button and set temperature to HIGH; press the "START/STOP" button. Heat sesame oil and sauté the leeks until they are just tender.
2. Add garlic, celery, carrot, and peppers; continue sautéing until they have softened, about 3 minutes.
3. Secure the lid and press the "SOUP" button. Press the "START/STOP" button; cook for 5 minutes at High pressure.
4. Once cooking is complete, use a quick pressure release and carefully remove the lid.
5. Next, puree soy sauce, raw cashews, and almond milk in your food processor or blender; process until creamy and uniform.
6. Stir this cream base into the soup; cook in the residual heat until everything is well incorporated. Let cool completely.

Storing

- Spoon your chowder into four airtight containers; keep in your refrigerator for up to 4 days.
- For freezing, place your chowder in heavy-duty freezer bags. When the bags are frozen through, stack them up like file folders to save space in the freezer.
- Freeze up to 4 months. Defrost in the microwave or refrigerator. Bon appétit!

77. French Green Lentils with Vegetables

There are many reasons to include lentils in your dietary regimen. Lentils are among the healthiest foods on the planet Earth. They can improve functions of the digestive system and cardiovascular system. They can also lower cholesterol levels and promote weight loss.

Servings 4

Ready in about 25 minutes

NUTRITIONAL INFORMATION (Per Serving)

183 - Calories
13.8g - Fat
13.7g - Carbs
3.5g - Protein
4g - Sugars

Ingredients

- 3 cups water
- 1 ½ cups dried French green lentils, rinsed
- 2 bay leaves
- A bunch of spring onions, roughly chopped
- 2 garlic cloves, minced
- 2 carrots, shredded
- 1 green bell pepper, thinly sliced
- 1 red bell pepper, thinly sliced
- 1/2 cup radishes, thinly sliced
- 1 cucumber, thinly sliced
- 1/4 cup extra-virgin olive oil
- 2 tablespoons balsamic vinegar
- 1/4 cup fresh basil, snipped
- 1 teaspoon mixed peppercorns, freshly cracked
- Sea salt, to taste

Directions

1. Place water, lentils, and bay leaves in your Crock-Pot Express.
2. Secure the lid and press the "SOUP" button. Press the "START/STOP" button; cook for 20 minutes at High pressure.
3. Once cooking is complete, use a quick pressure release and carefully remove the lid.
4. Drain green lentils and discard bay leaves; transfer to a large bowl.
5. Add spring onions, garlic, carrots, bell peppers, radishes, cucumber, olive oil, vinegar, and basil. Season with crushed peppercorns and sea salt. Toss to combine. Let cool completely.

Storing

- Spoon the lentil mixture into airtight containers or Ziploc bags; keep in your refrigerator for up to 5 to 7 days.
- For freezing, place the lentil mixture in airtight containers. Freeze up to 6 months. Defrost in the refrigerator. Bon appétit!

78. Kamut with Fresh Herbs and Green Olives

Nutty kamut goes well with fresh herbs, root vegetables, and olives. If you forgot to soak your kamut, just cook it on high pressure for 40 minutes.

Servings 4

Ready in about 25 minutes

NUTRITIONAL INFORMATION (Per Serving)

285 - Calories
5g - Fat
53.6g - Carbs
10.8g - Protein
7.4g - Sugars

Ingredients

- 1 tablespoon olive oil
- 2 shallots, chopped
- 2 cloves garlic minced
- 1 carrot, chopped
- 1 celery stalk, chopped
- 1 ½ cups kamut, soaked overnight
- 3 cups water
- Salt and black pepper, to taste
- 1/2 teaspoon dried rosemary
- 1/4 cup fresh chives, chopped
- 1/4 cup fresh parsley, chopped
- 1/2 cup green olives, pitted and sliced

Directions

1. Press the "BROWN/SAUTÉ" button and set temperature to HIGH; press the "START/STOP" button. Now, heat the oil until sizzling; sauté the shallots for 2 minutes or until tender.
2. Next, stir in the garlic, carrots and celery; continue to sauté until they are tender. Add kamut, water, salt, black pepper, and rosemary to the Crock-Pot Express.
3. Secure the lid and press the "MULTIGRAIN" button. Press the "START/STOP" button; cook for 20 minutes at High pressure.
4. Once cooking is complete, use a natural pressure release and carefully remove the lid. Add chives, parsley and olives. Let cool completely.

Storing

- Spoon cooked kamut into airtight containers or Ziploc bags; keep in your refrigerator for up to 4 to 6 days.
- For freezing, place cooked kamut in airtight containers. Freeze up to 6 months. Defrost in the refrigerator. Bon appétit!

79. Traditional Frijoles Colombianos

These Colombian-style beans also known as Frijoles Colombianos is a common dish from the Antioquia region. You can use cranberry beans as well.

Servings 5

Ready in about 35 minutes

NUTRITIONAL INFORMATION (Per Serving)

553 - Calories
5.2g - Fat
93.3g - Carbs
37.2g - Protein
8.5g - Sugars

Ingredients

- 1 tablespoon olive oil
- 1 purple onion, chopped
- 2 bell peppers, seeded and chopped
- 1 serrano pepper, seeded and minced
- 2 garlic cloves, minced
- 1/2 green plantain, cut into slices
- 1 ½ pounds dry Borlotti beans
- 4 cups roasted vegetable broth
- 2 ripe tomatoes, puréed
- 1/2 teaspoon cumin
- 1/2 teaspoon dried basil
- 1/2 teaspoon oregano
- Salt and freshly ground black pepper, to taste
- 1 heaping tablespoon fresh parsley leaves, chopped
- 2 bay leaves

Directions

1. Press the "BROWN/SAUTÉ" button and set temperature to HIGH; press the "START/STOP" button. Now, heat the oil until sizzling; sauté the onion for 2 minutes or until tender.
2. Then, add the peppers, garlic, and plantain; continue to sauté an additional minute or until they are fragrant; reserve.
3. Add the remaining ingredients to your Crock-Pot Express; stir to combine.
4. Secure the lid and press the "BEANS/CHILI" button. Press the "START/STOP" button; cook for 25 minutes at High pressure.
5. Once cooking is complete, use a natural pressure release and carefully remove the lid.
6. Add the reserved onion/pepper mixture. Seal the lid and let it sit for 5 minutes more or until everything is thoroughly warmed.
7. Discard bay leaves and taste for salt. Let cool completely.

Storing

- Spoon cooked beans into airtight containers or Ziploc bags; keep in your refrigerator for up to 3 to 4 days.
- For freezing, place cooked beans in airtight containers. It will maintain the best quality for about 4 to 6 months. Defrost in the refrigerator. Bon appétit!

80. Cabbage with Chanterelle Mushrooms

You deserve more than boring vegetables. Chanterelle mushrooms are a powerhouse of protein, vitamin B6, thiamine, selenium, manganese, and copper.

Servings 4

Ready in about 15 minutes

NUTRITIONAL INFORMATION (Per Serving)

121 - Calories
3.8g - Fat
20.3g - Carbs
4g - Protein
10.1g - Sugars

Ingredients

- 3 teaspoons olive oil
- 1/2 pound Chanterelle mushrooms, thinly sliced
- 1 pound purple cabbage, cut into wedges
- 2 red onions, cut into wedges
- 2 garlic cloves, smashed
- 1/3 cup Worcestershire sauce
- 2 tablespoons champagne vinegar
- 1 teaspoon cayenne pepper
- Salt, to taste
- 1/2 teaspoon ground bay leaf
- 1/3 teaspoon white pepper
- 1/2 teaspoon adobo seasoning

Directions

1. Press the "BROWN/SAUTÉ" button and set temperature to HIGH. Press the "START/STOP" button; heat the oil. Once hot, add the mushrooms; cook until they are lightly browned, about 4 minutes.
2. Add the other ingredients in the order listed above. Gently stir to combine and secure the lid.
3. Secure the lid and press the "SOUP" button. Press the "START/STOP" button; cook for 5 minutes at High pressure.
4. Once cooking is complete, use a quick pressure release and carefully remove the lid. Let cool completely.

Storing

- Place the cabbage and mushrooms in airtight containers or Ziploc bags; keep in your refrigerator for 3 to 5 days.
- Place the cabbage and mushrooms in freezable containers; they can be frozen for up to 10 months. Defrost in the refrigerator or microwave. Bon appétit!

FAST SNACKS & APPETIZERS

81. Sticky Glazed Mushrooms

With their natural umami taste, mushrooms go wonderfully with tangy and sweet hoisin sauce. You can also use King Trumpet mushrooms in this recipe.

Servings 5

Ready in about 10 minutes

NUTRITIONAL INFORMATION (Per Serving)

124 - Calories
8.1g - Fat
10.2g - Carbs
4.4g - Protein
7.7g - Sugars

Ingredients

- 20 ounces fresh white mushrooms
- 1/3 cup water
- 1 tablespoon apple cider vinegar
- 3 tablespoons soy sauce
- 1 tablespoon peanut butter
- 1 tablespoon molasses
- 2 garlic cloves, minced
- 2 tablespoons olive oil
- 1/2 teaspoon hot sauce
- Sea salt and ground black pepper, to taste
- 1 teaspoon paprika

Directions

1. Add all ingredients to your Crock-Pot Express.
2. Secure the lid and press the "SOUP" button. Press the "START/STOP" button; cook for 5 minutes at High pressure.
3. Once cooking is complete, use a quick pressure release and carefully remove the lid.
4. Remove the mushrooms from the cooking liquid.
5. Press the "BROWN/SAUTÉ" button and continue to simmer until the sauce has reduced and thickened.
6. Add the reserved mushrooms and toss to combine. Let cool completely.

Storing

- Place the mushrooms in airtight containers; keep in your refrigerator for 3 to 5 days.
- Place the mushrooms on the parchment-lined baking sheet, about 1-inch apart from each other; freeze for about 2 to 3 hours.
- Remove frozen mushrooms to a plastic freezer bag for long-term storage; they will maintain the best quality for 10 to 12 months.

82. Party Baby Carrots

Make delicate baby carrots for the next family gathering. In this recipe, the herbs are actually sautéed with coconut oil for an extra flavor!

Servings 6

Ready in about 15 minutes

NUTRITIONAL INFORMATION (Per Serving)

151 - Calories
4.8g - Fat
28g - Carbs
1.3g - Protein
21.1g - Sugars

Ingredients

- 1 ½ cups water
- 2 ½ pounds baby carrots, trimmed
- 1 teaspoon thyme
- 1 teaspoon dill
- Salt and white pepper, to taste
- 2 tablespoons coconut oil
- 1/4 cup honey

Directions

1. Add 1 ½ cups of water to the base of your Crock-Pot Express.
2. Now, arrange baby carrots in the steaming basket. Transfer the steaming basket to the Crock-Pot Express.
3. Secure the lid and press the "STEAM" button. Press the "START/STOP" button; cook for 3 minutes at High pressure.
4. Once cooking is complete, a quick pressure release and carefully remove the lid. Strain baby carrots and reserve.
5. Then, add the other ingredients to the Crock-Pot Express. Press the "BROWN/SAUTÉ" button and cook until everything is heated through. Add reserved baby carrots and gently stir.
6. Let cool completely.

Storing

- Place the carrots in airtight containers or Ziploc bags; keep in your refrigerator for up to 3 to 5 days.
- For freezing, place the carrots in airtight containers. It will maintain the best quality for about 10 to 12 months. Defrost in the refrigerator. Bon appétit!

83. Classic Artichoke Dipping Sauce

Make your party much better with this traditional version of cheese-artichoke dip. A quick and easy dipping sauce that is also freezer-friendly!

Servings 8

Ready in about 15 minutes

NUTRITIONAL INFORMATION (Per Serving)

190 - Calories
13.2g - Fat
8.3g - Carbs
10.3g - Protein
1g - Sugars

Ingredients

- 12 ounces canned artichoke hearts, chopped
- 2 cups kale, chopped
- 1 cup Ricotta cheese
- 1 ¼ cups Romano cheese, grated
- 1/2 cup mayonnaise
- 1 teaspoon gourmet mustard
- Salt and ground black pepper, to taste
- 1 teaspoon garlic powder
- 1/2 teaspoon shallot powder
- 1/2 teaspoon cumin powder

Directions

1. Lightly grease a baking pan that fits inside your Crock-Pot Express. Add all of the above ingredients and stir to combine well.
2. Add a metal rack and 1 ½ cups of water to the Crock-Pot Express.
3. Then, create a foil sling and place it on a rack; lower the baking pan onto the foil.
4. Secure the lid and press the "SOUP" button. Press the "START/STOP" button; cook for 9 minutes at High pressure.
5. Once cooking is complete, use a quick pressure release and carefully remove the lid. Let cool completely.

Storing

- Spoon your dip into airtight containers; keep in your refrigerator for up to 4 to 7 days.
- For freezing, place your dip in airtight containers or heavy-duty freezer bags. It will maintain the best quality for about 3 to 4 months. Defrost in the refrigerator. Enjoy!

84. Spicy Deviled Eggs with Chives

Here's a party favorite! Chives and mustard add an extra zing!

Servings 8

Ready in about 20 minutes

NUTRITIONAL INFORMATION (Per Serving)

138 - Calories
10.4g - Fat
1.2g - Carbs
9.1g - Protein
0.7g - Sugars

Ingredients

- 1 ½ cups water
- 8 eggs
- 3 teaspoons mayonnaise
- 1 tablespoon sour cream
- 1 teaspoon gourmet mustard
- 1/2 teaspoon hot sauce
- 1/3 teaspoon ground black pepper
- Crunchy sea salt, to taste
- 3 tablespoons fresh chives, thinly sliced

Directions

1. Pour the water into the base of your Crock-Pot Express.
2. Now, arrange eggs in the steaming basket. Transfer the steaming basket to the Crock-Pot Express.
3. Secure the lid and press the "BEANS/CHILI" button. Press the "START/STOP" button; cook for 5 minutes at High pressure.
4. Once cooking is complete, use a natural pressure release and carefully remove the lid.
5. Peel the eggs under running water. Remove the yolks and smash them with a fork; reserve.
6. Now, mix mayonnaise, sour cream, gourmet mustard, hot sauce, black pepper, and salt; add reserved yolks and mash everything.
7. Fill whites with this mixture, heaping it lightly. Garnish with fresh chives and place in the refrigerator to cool completely.

Storing

- Place deviled eggs in an airtight container or Ziploc bag; transfer to your refrigerator; they should be consumed within 2 days.
- For freezing, spoon out the yolk mixture from the deviled eggs. Add the egg yolk mixture to an airtight container or Ziploc bag.
- Place the container in the freezer for up to 3 months. To defrost, let them sit overnight in the refrigerator until they are fully thawed out.

85. Italian-Style Cheese Dip

When you need to get fancy with a party sauce, this Italian-style recipe is here to help. You can use Provolone and Fontina d'Aosta as well.

Servings 10

Ready in about 10 minutes

NUTRITIONAL INFORMATION (Per Serving)

209 - Calories
11.4g - Fat
5.3g - Carbs
21.1g - Protein
3.3g - Sugars

Ingredients

- 8 ounces Asiago cheese, grated
- 9 ounces Mozzarella cheese, crumbled
- 2 ripe Roma tomatoes, puréed
- 8 ounces pancetta, chopped
- 1/2 cup green olives, pitted and halved
- 1 bell pepper, chopped
- 1 teaspoon garlic powder
- 1 teaspoon shallot powder
- 1 teaspoon porcini powder
- 1 teaspoon dried oregano
- 1 teaspoon dried basil
- 1 teaspoon dried marjoram
- 2/3 cup beef bone broth
- 6 ounces Parmigiano-Reggiano cheese, grated

Directions

1. Combine all ingredients, except for Parmigiano-Reggiano cheese, in your Crock-Pot Express.
2. Secure the lid and press the "BEANS/CHILI" button. Press the "START/STOP" button; cook for 5 minutes at High pressure.
3. Once cooking is complete, use a quick pressure release and carefully remove the lid.
4. Top with Parmigiano-Reggiano cheese; cover and allow it to sit in the residual heat until cheese is melted. Let cool completely.

Storing

- Spoon your dip into airtight containers; keep in your refrigerator for up to 4 to 7 days.
- For freezing, place your dip in airtight containers or heavy-duty freezer bags. It will maintain the best quality for about 3 to 4 months. Defrost in the refrigerator. Enjoy!

86. Spicy Sausage and Cheese Dip

Packed full of goodness, this dipping sauce features hot breakfast sausage, tomatoes, and green chiles. Processed cheese adds a completely new dimension to the dip. Enjoy!

Servings 10

Ready in about 15 minutes

NUTRITIONAL INFORMATION (Per Serving)

295 - Calories
24.2g - Fat
10.1g - Carbs
13g - Protein
2.4g - Sugars

Ingredients

- 1 pound hot breakfast sausage, ground
- 2 shallots, chopped
- 2 cloves garlic, minced
- 2 cups tomatoes, pureed
- 2 cans green chiles, chopped
- 1 cup broth
- 1 pound block processed cheese

Directions

1. Press the "BROWN/SAUTÉ" button and set temperature to HIGH. Press the "START/STOP" button. Now, cook ground sausage with shallots.
2. Stir in garlic and cook 30 seconds more, stirring frequently. Add the tomatoes, green chiles, and broth.
3. Secure the lid and press the "SOUP" button. Press the "START/STOP" button; cook for 5 minutes at High pressure.
4. Once cooking is complete, use a quick pressure release and carefully remove the lid. Add block processed cheese and stir until it has melted. Let cool completely.

Storing

- Spoon your dip into airtight containers; keep in your refrigerator for up to 4 to 6 days.
- For freezing, place your dip in airtight containers or heavy-duty freezer bags. It will maintain the best quality for about 3 months. Defrost in the refrigerator. Enjoy!

87. Cheesy Broccoli Bites

Looking for more creative ways to eat broccoli? These bites are perfect for Saturday night with friends.

Servings 8

Ready in about 30 minutes

NUTRITIONAL INFORMATION (Per Serving)

142 - Calories
8.1g - Fat
9.6g - Carbs
9.5g - Protein
2.7g - Sugars

Ingredients

- 1 head of broccoli, broken into florets
- 1 ½ cups water
- 1 white onion, minced
- 1 garlic clove, minced
- 2 eggs, beaten
- 1 cup Colby cheese, grated
- 1 tablespoon fresh parsley, chopped
- 1 tablespoon fresh coriander, chopped
- Sea salt and ground black pepper, to taste

Directions

1. Add 1 cup of water and a steamer basket to the bottom of your Crock-Pot Express. Place broccoli florets in the steamer basket.
2. Secure the lid and press the "STEAM" button. Press the "START/STOP" button; cook for 6 minutes at High pressure.
3. Once cooking is complete, a quick pressure release and carefully remove the lid.
4. Allow broccoli florets to cool completely; then, add the remaining ingredients.
5. Mash the mixture and shape into tots with oiled hands.
6. Place broccoli tots on a lightly greased baking sheet. Bake in the preheated oven at 390 degrees F approximately 18 to 20 minutes, flipping them once. Let cool completely.

Storing

- Transfer the broccoli tots to the airtight containers and place in your refrigerator for up to 3 days.
- For freezing, place in freezer safe containers and freeze up to 1 month. Defrost in the microwave for a few minutes.

88. Mom's Vegetable and Tahini Dip

Gently cooked chunky vegetables and naturally tender, silky tahini are smartly paired in this amazing sauce for dipping.

Servings 8

Ready in about 10 minutes

NUTRITIONAL INFORMATION (Per Serving)

77 - Calories
5.5g - Fat
5.9g - Carbs
2.9g - Protein
1.7g - Sugars

Ingredients

- 1 ½ cups water
- 1 head cauliflower, cut into florets
- 1 cup broccoli, cut into florets
- 1 celery, sliced
- 1 carrot, sliced
- 1/3 cup tahini
- 2 tomatoes, pureed
- 1 serrano pepper, chopped
- 2 bell pepper, chopped
- 2 garlic cloves, chopped
- Salt and ground black pepper, to taste
- 1 teaspoon onion powder
- 1/2 teaspoon cayenne pepper
- 1/2 teaspoon cumin powder

Directions

1. Add the water, cauliflower, broccoli, celery, and carrot to your Crock-Pot Express.
2. Secure the lid and press the "STEAM" button. Press the "START/STOP" button; cook for 3 minutes at High pressure.
3. Once cooking is complete, a quick pressure release and carefully remove the lid.
4. Then, drain excess water out of vegetables. Transfer to a food processor and add the other ingredients.
5. Blend until everything is well incorporated. Let cool completely.

Storing

- Spoon your dip into airtight containers; keep in your refrigerator for up to 4 to 7 days.
- For freezing, place your dip in airtight containers or heavy-duty freezer bags. It will maintain the best quality for about 3 to 4 months. Defrost in the refrigerator. Bon appétit!

89. Asian-Style Short Ribs

Looking for the perfect appetizer for your next summer party? Try these fall-off-the-bone ribs with a Korean flair.

Servings 6

Ready in about 1 hour 5 minutes

NUTRITIONAL INFORMATION (Per Serving)

250 - Calories
13.1g - Fat
7.9g - Carbs
24.1g - Protein
6.2g - Sugars

Ingredients

- 2 pounds Korean-style beef short ribs
- 1 Asian pear, peeled and grated
- 2 tablespoons brown sugar
- 1/2 teaspoon salt
- 1/3 teaspoon ground black pepper
- 1 teaspoon granulated garlic
- 1/2 cup water
- 1/2 cup soy sauce
- 1/4 cup mirin
- 1 teaspoon liquid smoke

Directions

1. Add all of the above ingredients to your Crock-Pot Express.
2. Secure the lid and press the "MEAT/STEW" button. Press the "START/STOP" button; cook for 60 minutes at High pressure.
3. Once cooking is complete, use a natural pressure release and carefully remove the lid. Cut ribs, slicing between bones. Let cool completely.

Storing

- Divide ribs into three portions. Place each portion of ribs in an airtight container; keep in your refrigerator for 3 to 5 days.
- For freezing, place the ribs in airtight containers or heavy-duty freezer bags. Freeze up to 4 to 6 months.
- Defrost in the refrigerator. Reheat in your oven at 250 degrees F until heated through. Bon appétit!

90. Classic Spicy Cocktail Wieners

Little wieners are cooked in a tangy barbeque sauce with jalapenos and yellow onion. Great snack for cocktail parties and entertaining!

Servings 12

Ready in about 10 minutes

NUTRITIONAL INFORMATION (Per Serving)

333 - Calories
23.4g - Fat
19.6g - Carbs
10g - Protein
13.2g - Sugars

Ingredients

- 2 (16-ounce) packages little wieners
- 1/2 (18-ounce) bottle barbeque sauce
- 1/2 cup ketchup
- 3 tablespoons honey
- 1/2 yellow onion, chopped
- 2 jalapenos, sliced
- 1 teaspoon garlic powder
- 1 teaspoon cumin powder
- 1/2 teaspoon mustard powder

Directions

1. Add little wieners, barbecue sauce, ketchup, honey, onion, jalapenos, garlic powder, cumin, and mustard powder to the Crock-Pot Express. Stir to combine well.
2. Secure the lid and press the "STEAM" button. Press the "START/STOP" button; cook for 3 minutes at High pressure.
3. Once cooking is complete, use a natural pressure release and carefully remove the lid. You can thicken the sauce if desired. Let cool completely.

Storing

- Transfer the little wieners to the airtight containers and place in your refrigerator for up to 3 to 4 days.
- For freezing, place the little wieners in freezer safe containers or wrap tightly with heavy-duty aluminum foil; freeze up to 1 to 2 months. Defrost in the microwave for a few minutes. Enjoy!

DESSERTS

91. Father's Day Mug Cakes

With its luscious flavor and gooey texture, chocolate mug cakes will blow your mind! They are easy to whip up in the Crock-Pot Express.

Servings 2

Ready in about 15 minutes

NUTRITIONAL INFORMATION (Per Serving)

268 - Calories
10.5g - Fat
34.8g - Carbs
10.6g - Protein
31.1g - Sugars

Ingredients

- 1/2 cup coconut flour
- 2 eggs
- 2 tablespoons honey
- 1 teaspoon vanilla
- 1/4 teaspoon grated nutmeg
- 1 tablespoon cocoa powder
- 1 medium-sized mango, peeled and diced

Directions

1. Combine the coconut flour, eggs, honey, vanilla, nutmeg and cocoa powder in two lightly greased mugs.
2. Then, add 1 cup of water and a metal trivet to the Crock-Pot Express. Lower the uncovered mugs onto the trivet.
3. Secure the lid and press the "DESSERT" button. Press the "START/STOP" button; cook for 10 minutes at High pressure.
4. Once cooking is complete, use a quick pressure release and carefully remove the lid. Top with diced mango. Let cool completely.

Storing

- Divide your cakes between two airtight containers; keep in the refrigerator for 3 to 4 days.
- For freezing, divide your cakes among four Ziploc bags and freeze up to 4 to 5 months. Defrost in your microwave for a couple of minutes. Enjoy!

92. Luxury Dessert with Cream and Apricots

Crock-Pot Express desserts mean less fuss and more spare time! It will be hard to say No to this bread pudding with succulent dried apricots, fresh milk and flavorful cream.

Servings 6

Ready in about 20 minutes

NUTRITIONAL INFORMATION (Per Serving)

410 - Calories
24.3g - Fat
37.4g - Carbs
11.5g - Protein
25.6g - Sugars

Ingredients
- 4 cups Italian bread, cubed
- 1/2 cup granulated sugar
- 2 tablespoons molasses
- 1/2 cup dried apricots, soaked and chopped
- 2 tablespoons coconut oil
- 1 teaspoon vanilla paste
- A pinch of grated nutmeg
- A pinch of salt
- 1 teaspoon cinnamon, ground
- 1/2 teaspoon star anise, ground
- 2 cups milk
- 4 eggs, whisked
- 1 1/3 cups heavy cream

Directions

1. Add 1 ½ cups of water and a metal rack to the Crock-Pot Express.
2. Grease a baking dish with a nonstick cooking spray. Throw bread cubes into the prepared baking dish.
3. In a mixing bowl, thoroughly combine the remaining ingredients. Pour the mixture over the bread cubes. Cover with a piece of foil, making a foil sling.
4. Secure the lid and press the "DESSERT" button. Press the "START/ STOP" button; cook for 15 minutes at High pressure.
5. Once cooking is complete, use a quick pressure release and carefully remove the lid. Let cool completely.

Storing

- Spoon bread pudding into airtight containers; keep in your refrigerator for up to 5 to 6 days.
- For freezing, place bread pudding in airtight containers or heavy-duty freezer bags. It will maintain the best quality for about 2 to 3 months. Defrost in your refrigerator. Bon appétit!

93. Crunchy Chocolate Bars with Cranberries

Oats are not just breakfast cereals; they also make a great, luscious dessert. These bars are great to serve at gatherings

Servings 8

Ready in about 20 minutes

NUTRITIONAL INFORMATION (Per Serving)

201 - Calories
7.3g - Fat
27.2g - Carbs
6.9g - Protein
11.8g - Sugars

Ingredients

- 3 eggs, whisked
- 1/2 cup sour cream
- 1/4 cup honey
- 2 teaspoons coconut oil, melted
- 1/2 teaspoon rum extract
- 1/2 teaspoon vanilla extract
- 3/4 cup quick oats, pudding-y
- 1/3 cup all-purpose flour
- 1 teaspoon baking soda
- 1 teaspoon baking powder
- 1/2 teaspoon cardamom
- 1/2 teaspoon cinnamon
- 1 cup dark chocolate chips
- A pinch of kosher salt
- 3/4 cup cranberries

Directions

1. Add 1 cup of water and a metal trivet to the Crock-Pot Express. Now, spritz a baking pan with a nonstick cooking spray.
2. In a mixing bowl, whisk the eggs, sour cream, honey, coconut oil, rum extract, and vanilla extract.
3. Add oats, flour, baking soda, baking powder, cardamom, cinnamon, salt, and chocolate chips; stir until everything is well incorporated. After that, fold in cranberries.
4. Scrape the batter into the baking pan.
5. Secure the lid and press the "DESSERT" button. Press the "START/ STOP" button; cook for 12 minutes at High pressure.
6. Once cooking is complete, use a natural pressure release and carefully remove the lid.
7. Let cool completely.

Storing

- Place chocolate bars in airtight containers; keep in your refrigerator for 4 to 5 days.
- To freeze, place chocolate bars in airtight containers or Ziploc bags; it can be frozen for 6 months. Defrost in your microwave for a few minutes. Bon appétit!

94. Valentine's Day Coconut Cheesecake

The Crock-Pot Express makes fantastic cheesecake, cooking it equally all the way through! The steam will make it extra fluffy and flavorful.

Servings 10

Ready in about 1 hour + freezing time

NUTRITIONAL INFORMATION (Per Serving)

487 - Calories
33.5g - Fat
39.1g - Carbs
8.7g - Protein
28.2g - Sugars

Ingredients

- 1 ½ cups vanilla sugar cookies, crumbled
- 1/2 stick butter, melted
- For the Filling:
- 22 ounces cream cheese, room temperature
- 3/4 cup granulated sugar
- 1 ½ tablespoons cornstarch
- 2 eggs, room temperature
- 1/3 cup sour cream
- 1/2 teaspoon coconut extract
- 1/2 teaspoon pure anise extract
- 1/4 teaspoon freshly grated nutmeg
- 6 ounces semisweet chocolate chips
- 3 ounces sweetened shredded coconut

Directions

1. Lightly oil a baking pan that fits in your Crock-Pot Express. Cover the bottom with a baking paper.
2. Thoroughly combine crumbled cookies with melted butter; now, press the crust into the baking pan and transfer to your freezer.
3. Next, beat the cream cheese with a mixer on low speed. Stir in the sugar and cornstarch and continue mixing on low speed until everything is uniform and smooth.
4. Fold in the eggs, one at a time, and continue to beat with the mixer. Now, stir in sour cream, coconut extract, anise extract, and nutmeg; mix again.
5. Then, microwave the chocolate chips about 1 minute, stirring once or twice. Add the melted chocolate to the cheesecake batter; add shredded coconut and stir to combine.
6. Pour the chocolate mixture into the baking pan on top of the crust.
7. Add 1 cup of water and trivet to the Crock-Pot Express. Lower the prepared pan onto the trivet and secure the lid.
8. Secure the lid and press the "DESSERT" button. Press the "START/STOP" button; cook for 40 minutes at High pressure.
9. Once cooking is complete, use a natural pressure release and carefully remove the lid. Allow your cheesecake to cool completely.

Storing

- Refrigerate your cheesecake covered loosely with plastic wrap. Keep in your refrigerator for up to 7 days.
- To freeze, wrap cheesecake tightly with foil or place in heavy-duty freezer bag; freeze for about 2 to 3 months. Bon appétit!

95. Orange-Coconut Mini Cheesecakes

If you have a sweet tooth, this is a must-try dessert recipe for Crock-Pot Express. You can serve it with fresh or frozen berries, pineapple od banana.

Servings 4

Ready in about 15 minutes

NUTRITIONAL INFORMATION (Per Serving)

425 - Calories
33.6g - Fat
20.2g - Carbs
11.4g - Protein
16.7g - Sugars

Ingredients

- 12 ounces cream cheese
- 2 ounces sour cream
- 1/3 cup coconut sugar
- 1/2 teaspoon vanilla extract
- 1/2 teaspoon coconut extract
- 1 teaspoon orange zest
- 1/2 cup coconut flakes
- 2 eggs
- 4 tablespoons orange curd

Directions

1. Start by adding 1 ½ cups of water and a metal trivet to the bottom of the Crock-Pot Express.
2. In a mixing bowl, combine cream cheese, sour cream, coconut sugar, vanilla, coconut extract, and orange zest.
3. Now, add coconut flakes and eggs; whisk until everything is well combined.
4. Divide the batter between four jars. Top with orange curd. Lower the jars onto the trivet. Now, cover your jars with foil.
5. Secure the lid and press the "DESSERT" button. Press the "START/STOP" button; cook for 9 minutes at High pressure.
6. Once cooking is complete, use a natural pressure release and carefully remove the lid. Let cool completely.

Storing

- Refrigerate mini cheesecakes covered loosely with plastic wrap. Keep in your refrigerator for up to 7 days.
- To freeze, wrap mini cheesecakes tightly with foil or place in heavy-duty freezer bag; freeze for about 2 to 3 months. Bon appétit!

96. Fancy Shortbread Cake

You can store leftover cake at room temperature for several days. It also freezes well.

Servings 10

Ready in about 35 minutes

NUTRITIONAL INFORMATION (Per Serving)

200 - Calories
10.9g - Fat
18.7g - Carbs
6.9g - Protein
9.2g - Sugars

Ingredients

- Nonstick cooking spray
- 4 eggs, beaten
- 1/3 cup sugar
- 1 tablespoon coconut oil, softened
- 1/2 cup full-fat cream cheese
- 1 cup sour cream
- 1 teaspoon vanilla extract
- 1/2 teaspoon cardamom
- 3/4 cup whole wheat flour
- A pinch of coarse salt
- 1 teaspoon baking soda
- 1 teaspoon baking powder
- Sour Cream Glaze:
- 1/2 cup sour cream
- 1/2 cup powdered sugar
- 1 teaspoon vanilla extract

Directions

1. Prepare your Crock-Pot Express by adding 1 cup of water and a metal rack to its bottom. Spritz a bundt pan with a nonstick cooking spray.
2. Then, whisk the eggs and sugar until creamy and pale. Add the coconut oil, cheese, sour cream, vanilla, and cardamom; beat until everything is well incorporated.
3. In another mixing bowl, thoroughly combine the flour with salt, baking soda, and baking powder. Add the flour mixture to the egg mixture. Spoon the batter into the prepared pan. Lower the pan onto the rack.
4. Secure the lid and press the "DESSERT" button. Press the "START/STOP" button; cook for 25 minutes at High pressure.
5. Once cooking is complete, use a natural pressure release and carefully remove the lid.
6. Meanwhile, make the glaze by whisking sour cream, powdered sugar, and vanilla. Brush the cake with glaze and place in your refrigerator. Let cool completely.

Storing

- Cover your cake with foil or plastic wrap to prevent drying out; it will last for about 1 to 2 days at room temperature.
- Cover your cake loosely with aluminum foil or plastic wrap and refrigerate for 7 days.
- To freeze, wrap your cake tightly with aluminum foil or plastic freezer wrap, or place in heavy-duty freezer bag; freeze for about 4 to 5 months. Enjoy!

97. St Patrick's Day Whiskey Pudding

A simple bread pudding is arguably the most convenient choice when it comes to the Crock-Pot Express deserts. This recipe calls for Brioche but feel free to use Challah or Pullman loaf.

Servings 8

Ready in about 2 hours 45 minutes

NUTRITIONAL INFORMATION (Per Serving)

352 - Calories
13.2g - Fat
43.9g - Carbs
14.2g - Protein
10.1g - Sugars

Ingredients

- 1 loaf Brioche bread, cubed
- 2 ½ cups milk
- 4 eggs, beaten
- 1 teaspoon vanilla extract
- 1/2 teaspoon coconut extract
- 1/4 cup coconut oil, melted
- 4 tablespoons agave syrup
- 1/4 cup bourbon whiskey

Directions

1. Place the bread in a baking dish that is previously greased with a nonstick cooking spray.
2. Then, in another bowl, thoroughly combine the milk, eggs, vanilla, coconut extract, coconut oil, agave syrup, and bourbon whiskey.
3. Pour the milk/bourbon mixture over the bread; press with a wide spatula to soak and place in the refrigerator for 1 to 2 hours.
4. Add 1 ½ cups of water and a metal trivet to your Crock-Pot Express. Lower the baking dish onto the trivet.
5. Secure the lid and press the "DESSERT" button. Press the "START/STOP" button; cook for 35 minutes at High pressure.
6. Once cooking is complete, use a quick pressure release and carefully remove the lid. Let cool completely.

Storing

- Spoon bread pudding into airtight containers; keep in your refrigerator for up to 5 to 6 days.
- For freezing, place bread pudding in airtight containers or heavy-duty freezer bags. It will maintain the best quality for about 2 to 3 months. Defrost in your refrigerator. Bon appétit!

98. Autumn Cake with Cream Cheese Frosting

Inspired by pumpkin purée, you can come up with a dessert that literally melts in your mouth! When you are just not in the mood to cook, it's good to have a can of pumpkin purée on hand.

Servings 10

Ready in about 25 minutes + chilling time

NUTRITIONAL INFORMATION (Per Serving)

357 - Calories
15.2g - Fat
52.6g - Carbs
4.1g - Protein
34.9g - Sugars

Ingredients

Batter:
- 2 cups pumpkin purée
- 3/4 cup applesauce
- 1 cup granulated sugar
- 1 tablespoon molasses
- 1/2 teaspoon crystallized ginger
- 1/8 teaspoon salt
- 1/8 teaspoon grated nutmeg
- 1/4 teaspoon cardamom, ground
- 1/2 teaspoon cinnamon, ground
- 1 teaspoon vanilla extract
- 1 ½ cups all-purpose flour
- 1 teaspoon baking powder

Cream Cheese Frosting:
- 7 ounces cream cheese, at room temperature
- 1 stick butter, at room temperature
- 2 cups powdered sugar

Directions

1. In a mixing bowl, combine all dry ingredients for the batter. Then, in a separate mixing bowl, thoroughly combine all wet ingredients.
2. Then, add wet mixture to the dry mixture; pour the batter into a cake pan that is previously greased with melted butter.
3. Add 1 ½ cups of water and metal trivet to the Crock-Pot Express. Lower the cake pan onto the trivet.
4. Secure the lid and press the "DESSERT" button. Press the "START/STOP" button; cook for 20 minutes at High pressure.
5. Once cooking is complete, use a natural pressure release and carefully remove the lid.
6. Meanwhile, make the frosting. Beat the cream cheese and butter with an electric mixer on high speed. Add powdered sugar.
7. Continue to beat until the frosting has thickened. Spread the frosting on the cooled cake. Let cool completely.

Storing

- Refrigerate your cake covered loosely with plastic wrap. Keep in your refrigerator for up to 7 days.
- To freeze, wrap your cake tightly with foil or place in heavy-duty freezer bag; freeze for about 2 to 3 months. Bon appétit!

99. Grandma's Classic Cake

Here is an easy and stress-free way to make a family dessert. The simplest things are often the best! Grandma knows that!

Servings 6

Ready in about 45 minutes

NUTRITIONAL INFORMATION (Per Serving)

244 - Calories
17.3g - Fat
21.3g - Carbs
2.7g - Protein
18.8g - Sugars

Ingredients

- 1 ¼ cups coconut flour
- 1/4 cup walnuts, ground
- 1 ½ teaspoons baking powder
- 1 cup sugar
- 1 teaspoon ground cinnamon
- 1/2 teaspoon grated nutmeg
- 1 teaspoon orange zest, finely grated
- 1/4 teaspoon ground star anise
- 2 eggs plus 1 egg yolk, whisked
- 1/2 stick butter, at room temperature
- 3/4 cup double cream

Directions

1. Add 1 ½ cups of water and a steamer rack to your Crock-Pot Express. Spritz the inside of a baking pan with a nonstick cooking spray.
2. Thoroughly combine dry ingredients. Then, mix the wet ingredients. Add the wet mixture to the dry flour mixture and mix until everything is well incorporated.
3. Scrape the batter mixture into the prepared baking pan. Now, cover the baking pan with a piece of foil, making a foil sling.
4. Place the baking pan on the steamer rack and secure the lid.
5. Secure the lid and press the "DESSERT" button. Press the "START/ STOP" button; cook for 35 minutes at High pressure.
6. Once cooking is complete, use a natural pressure release and carefully remove the lid. Let cool completely.

Storing

- Refrigerate your cake covered loosely with plastic wrap. Keep in your refrigerator for up to 7 days.
- To freeze, wrap your cake tightly with foil or place in heavy-duty freezer bag; freeze for about 4 to 6 months. Bon appétit!

100. Easy Lava Molten Cake

Lava molten cake is one of the most popular desserts in the world. Now, you can make it in your Crock-Pot Express. Awesome!

Servings 8

Ready in about 20 minutes

NUTRITIONAL INFORMATION (Per Serving)

301 - Calories
15.4g - Fat
32.5g - Carbs
7.7g - Protein
26.1g - Sugars

Ingredients

- A nonstick cooking spray
- 1 tablespoon granulated sugar
- 1/4 cup butter, melted
- 3 eggs, beaten
- 1 teaspoon vanilla extract
- 1/2 teaspoon pure almond extract
- 1/4 teaspoon star anise, ground
- 1/4 teaspoon ground cinnamon
- 1/3 cup powdered sugar
- 3/4 cup canned dulce de leche
- 4 tablespoons all-purpose flour
- 1/8 teaspoon kosher salt

Directions

1. Spritz a cake pan with a nonstick cooking spray. Then, sprinkle the bottom of your pan with granulated sugar.
2. Beat the butter with eggs, vanilla, almond extract, star anise, and ground cinnamon. Add powdered sugar, canned dulce de leche, flour, and salt. Mix until a thick batter is achieved.
3. Scrape the batter into the prepared cake pan.
4. Place 1 cup of water and metal trivet in the Crock-Pot Express. Place the cake pan on the trivet.
5. Secure the lid and press the "DESSERT" button. Press the "START/STOP" button; cook for 10 minutes at High pressure.
6. Once cooking is complete, use a quick pressure release and carefully remove the lid. Let cool completely.

Storing

- Cover your cake with foil or plastic wrap to prevent drying out; it will last for about 1 to 2 days at room temperature.
- Cover your cake loosely with aluminum foil or plastic wrap and refrigerate for 7 days.
- To freeze, wrap your cake tightly with aluminum foil or plastic freezer wrap, or place in heavy-duty freezer bag; freeze for about 4 to 6 months. Enjoy!

101. Stewed Peaches in Wine Sauce

For this recipe, use a lighter and fruity white wine. Serve with a dollop of vanilla ice cream if desired.

Servings 4

Ready in about 15 minutes

NUTRITIONAL INFORMATION (Per Serving)

405 - Calories
0.8g - Fat
75.1g - Carbs
3g - Protein
67.8g - Sugars

Ingredients

- 8 firm peaches, cut into halves
- 1/2 orange, cut into rounds
- 1/2 lemon, cut into rounds
- 1/2 cup water
- 1/2 cup apple juice
- 1 bottle white wine
- 1 ½ cups sugar
- 2 cinnamon sticks
- 2 whole cloves
- 1 large vanilla bean pod, split open lengthwise
- 1 tablespoon crystallized ginger

Directions

1. Arrange peaches in the bottom of your Crock-Pot Express.
2. Mix the remaining ingredients until they are thoroughly combined. Add this poaching liquid to the Crock-Pot Express.
3. Secure the lid and press the "STEAM" button. Press the "START/STOP" button; cook for 3 minutes at High pressure.
4. Once cooking is complete, use a quick pressure release and carefully remove the lid. Remove the peaches from the Crock-Pot Express and set them aside.
5. Press the "BROWN/SAUTÉ" button and set temperature to HIGH. Now, press the "START/STOP" button and simmer the poaching liquid until reduced by half, about 10 minutes.
6. Let cool completely.

Storing

- Place the peaches and sauce in airtight containers; it can be stored in the refrigerator up to 2 weeks.
- Place the peaches and sauce in a heavy-duty freezer bag. Store in your freezer up to 8 to 10 months. Defrost in the refrigerator. Bon appétit!

102. Autumn Caramel and Fruit Crisp

This fruity dessert is perfect for autumn and winter, but you can also make it with peaches in the summer. To serve, drizzle caramel syrup over each serving.

Servings 6

Ready in about 25 minutes

NUTRITIONAL INFORMATION (Per Serving)

227 - Calories
8.1g - Fat
42.8g - Carbs
3.4g - Protein
28.1g - Sugars

Ingredients

- 2 pears, cored, peeled and sliced
- 10 plums, pitted and halved
- 3/4 cup rolled oats
- 3 tablespoons flour
- 1/4 cup sugar
- 2 tablespoons maple syrup
- 2 tablespoons caramel syrup, plus more for topping
- 2 tablespoons fresh orange juice
- 1 teaspoon ground cinnamon
- A pinch of salt
- 3 tablespoons coconut oil

Directions

1. Arrange pears and plums in the bottom of a lightly buttered baking pan.
2. In a mixing bowl, thoroughly combine rolled oats, flour, sugar, maple syrup, caramel syrup, orange juice, cinnamon, salt and coconut oil.
3. Top the prepared pears and plums with the oat layer. Now, distribute the oat layer evenly using a spatula.
4. Add 1 cup of water and a metal trivet to your Crock-Pot Express. Lower the baking pan onto the trivet. Cover with a sheet of foil.
5. Secure the lid and press the "DESSERT" button. Press the "START/STOP" button; cook for 10 minutes at High pressure.
6. Once cooking is complete, use a natural pressure release and carefully remove the lid. Remove the foil and let your crisp cool completely.

Storing

- Place the crisp in airtight containers; keep in your refrigerator for 4 to 5 days.
- To freeze, place the crisp in airtight containers or Ziploc bags; it can be frozen for 6 months. Defrost in your microwave for a few minutes. Bon appétit!

103. French Cheesecake with Almonds

Classic desserts deserve a comeback in every kitchen. This stunning cheesecake recipe features creamy and silky Neufchâtel cheese, super-healthy almonds and versatile graham cracker crumbs.

Servings 8

Ready in about 45 minutes

NUTRITIONAL INFORMATION (Per Serving)

445 - Calories
33.2g - Fat
15.3g - Carbs
21.2g - Protein
7.4g - Sugars

Ingredients

- 24 ounces Neufchâtel cheese
- 1 cup sour cream
- 5 eggs
- 1/4 cup flour
- 1/2 teaspoon pure vanilla extract
- 1/2 teaspoon pure almond extract
- 1 ½ cups graham cracker crumbs
- 1/2 cup almonds, roughly chopped
- 1/2 stick butter, melted

Directions

1. In a mixing bowl, beat Neufchâtel cheese with sour cream. Now, fold in eggs, one at a time.
2. Stir in the flour, vanilla extract, and almond extract; mix to combine well.
3. In a separate mixing bowl, thoroughly combine graham cracker crumbs, almonds, and butter. Press this crust mixture into a baking pan.
4. Pour the egg/cheese mixture into the pan. Cover with a sheet of foil; make sure that foil fits tightly around sides and under the bottom of your baking pan.
5. Secure the lid and press the "DESSERT" button. Press the "START/STOP" button; cook for 40 minutes at High pressure.
6. Once cooking is complete, use a quick pressure release and carefully remove the lid. Allow your cheesecake to cool completely.

Storing

- Refrigerate your cheesecake covered loosely with plastic wrap. Keep in your refrigerator for up to 7 days.
- To freeze, wrap cheesecake tightly with foil or place in heavy-duty freezer bag; freeze for about 2 to 3 months. Bon appétit!

104. Berry and Mango Compote

Looking for a light dessert to kick off your party dinner? We've got an amazing recipe that you will make in minutes. Place in your refrigerator until ready to serve and keep for up to 2 days.

Servings 6

Ready in about 15 minutes

NUTRITIONAL INFORMATION (Per Serving)

193 - Calories
0.4g - Fat
48.8g - Carbs
1.1g - Protein
44.5g - Sugars

Ingredients

- 1/2 pound blueberries
- 1/2 pound blackberries
- 1/2 pound mango, pitted and diced
- 1 cup Muscovado sugar
- 1 cinnamon stick
- 1 vanilla pod
- 1 teaspoon whole cloves
- 2 tablespoons orange juice
- 1 teaspoon orange zest

Directions

1. Add all of the above ingredients to your Crock-Pot Express.
2. Secure the lid and press the "STEAM" button. Press the "START/STOP" button; cook for 6 minutes at High pressure.
3. Once cooking is complete, use a natural pressure release and carefully remove the lid. Let cool completely.

Storing

- Place the compote in airtight containers; it can be stored in the refrigerator up to 2 weeks.
- Place the compote in a heavy-duty freezer bag. Store in your freezer up to 8 to 10 months. Defrost in the refrigerator. Bon appétit!

105. Mini Molten Cakes

These mini molten lava cakes are awesome! Dipping into that ooey-gooey middle is really great feeling!

Servings 6

Ready in about 20 minutes

NUTRITIONAL INFORMATION (Per Serving)

393 - Calories
21.1g - Fat
45.6g - Carbs
5.6g - Protein
35.4g - Sugars

Ingredients

- 1 stick butter
- 6 ounces butterscotch morsels
- 3/4 cup powdered sugar
- 3 eggs, whisked
- 1/2 teaspoon vanilla extract
- 7 tablespoons all-purpose flour
- A pinch of coarse salt

Directions

1. Add 1 ½ cups of water and a metal rack to the Crock-Pot Express. Line a standard-size muffin tin with muffin papers.
2. In a microwave-safe bowl, microwave butter and butterscotch morsels for about 40 seconds. Stir in powdered sugar.
3. Add the remaining ingredients. Spoon the batter into the prepared muffin tin.
4. Secure the lid and press the "DESSERT" button. Press the "START/STOP" button; cook for 10 minutes at High pressure.
5. Once cooking is complete, use a quick pressure release and carefully remove the lid.
6. To remove, let it cool for 5 to 6 minutes. Run a small knife around the sides of each cake and remove them from the muffin tin. Let cool completely.

Storing

- Cover your mini cakes loosely with aluminum foil or plastic wrap and refrigerate for 7 days.
- To freeze, wrap mini cakes tightly with aluminum foil or plastic freezer wrap, or place in heavy-duty freezer bag; freeze for about 4 to 6 months. Enjoy!

Made in the USA
Lexington, KY
04 November 2018